D1447385

Paths of Love

The Discernment of Vocation

According to the Teaching

of Aquinas, Ignatius, and Pope John Paul II

Joseph Bolin

Listen, O son, to the precepts of your master,
and incline the ear of your heart.

Rule of St. Benedict, Prologue

Table of Contents

Abbreviations

AAS: Acta Apostolicae Sedis
CCSL: Corpus Christianorum Series Latina
In Sent.: In Libros Sententiarum Petri Lombardi
SCG: Summa Contra Gentiles
ST: Summa Theologiae
PG: Patrologia Graeca
PL: Patrologia Latina

Acknowledgments

This work has its origin in an e-mail exchange with my brother, David Bolin (now Br. Thomas Bolin, OSB), on the subject of vocation. I came to see the value of St. Thomas Aquinas's approach to religious vocation, and defended Aquinas's position in my Bachelor's thesis for Thomas Aquinas College. In the following years, I continued reflecting on the topic of vocation. The present work on vocations is the fruit of this reflection.

In the first place, then, I thank Br. Thomas Bolin, for his inspiration, encouragement, and assistance. I have learned much through our many conversations about moral activity, the spiritual life, and vocation. He has also given many helpful comments as I wrote this work itself.

I thank also my teachers at the International Theological Institute, from whom I have learned a great deal that has borne fruit in this work. I mention especially Peter Kwasniewski, Walter Thompson, and Michael Waldstein.

My thanks go also to the many friends and confrères whose thoughts, ideas, and reactions have been helpful in writing this book. Though it is impossible to name everyone, worthy of special mention are my parents, Jeremy Holmes, Andrew Seeley, Deacon Joseph Levine, MaryAnn McGrath, Shannon McAlister, Matthew Fish, Thérèse Grimm, Bernadette Bartosch, and Katharina Fischer.

The translations of the Vatican and papal texts used in this book have been taken or adapted from the official translations as found on the Vatican website (where available). The translation of St. Francis de Sales' *Treatise on the Love of God* has been adapted from the translation by Rev. Henry Mackey. The translations of the spiritual exercises of St. Ignatius draw upon the translations made by Fr. Elder Mullan and Louis Puhl. The translations from the directories for the exercises are mostly adapted from the translation of Martin Palmer. Otherwise, all translations are my own. I am indebted to Grzegorz Ignatik for help in the translation of *Love and*

Responsibility, and to Andrei Goția for help with various questions regarding translation.

Finally I wish to thank those who have given their support in the pursuit of this study and writing, particularly Fr. Anthony Myers, Fr. Carlos Urrutigoity, and Fr. John Saward.

Joseph F. Bolin
June 24, 2008
Birth of John the Baptist

Introduction

"Good teacher, what must I do to inherit eternal life?"[1] (Mar 10:17) This question, asked of Jesus centuries ago, continues to be asked by Christians today. The answer to this question is one's "vocation." The ways in which one may ask this question, and the means by which one may seek an answer, are indeed many and diverse, according to the character of each person, and the workings and providence of God. Nonetheless, we can identify two basic ways of approaching the question, each of which has strengths and weaknesses peculiar to it. The first approach basically asks the question in this way: "What will bring me and others closest to God, and make us happiest?" The second approach asks it in a different way: "What does God most want me to do with my life?"

The fundamental distinction between these two approaches, and at the same time their complementarity, is often not sufficiently appreciated. Most treatments of vocation basically adopt one of these two approaches, and either disregard or reject the other one. We believe that a much sounder point of view will be attained by a balanced consideration of both approaches. In this work, then, we will examine these two basic ways of approaching the question of vocation, and the advantages and the potential dangers of each approach. Then based on these considerations, we will propose an integral view of vocations that seeks to preserve the benefits of each approach.

Most books on vocation fall into one of two categories: either they are theological treatises, of interest mostly to theology students and spiritual directors, or they are vocational guidebooks, which offer lots of practical advice on choosing one's vocation, but fail to provide substantial nourishment to their readers, to give them a solid foundation from which they can proceed further on

---

1 Except where otherwise noted, all scripture quotations are from the *Revised Standard Version, Catholic Edition* (San Francisco: Ignatius Press, 1966).

x

their own. This book is of a different kind. The goal of this book is neither to make an exhaustive theological treatment of vocation, nor to give detailed advice or a foolproof "method" for discerning one's vocation. Rather, its goal is to provide a deep, yet simple and accessible perspective on vocation, as it were a solid footing, both for individuals who are discerning their vocation, and for spiritual directors who are guiding others in the choice of a vocation.

In this work, we will seek to follow the twofold desire of the Church in regard to vocation—to promote the universal vocation to holiness, and to promote vocations to the priesthood and religious life as vocations that have a special value and irreplaceable role in the Church. The universal vocation to holiness has been described by Pope Paul VI as the "most characteristic element" of the Second Vatican Council's teaching.

> The Second Vatican Council again and again called all the faithful, of whatever condition or order, to the fullness of Christian life and the perfection of charity; this exhortation to holiness may be considered the most characteristic element of the council's teaching, and as its final goal.[2]

But at the same time, the popes note the importance of manifesting the special value and character of the priestly and religious life, as may be seen in the following text of Pope John Paul II, where he simultaneously points to the universal vocation to holiness, and to the special value of the priesthood and religious life:

> It is indeed fitting to emphasize over and over again the *universal vocation to holiness* of the whole People of God.... An integral part of Christian family life is the inculcation in its members of *an appreciation of the priesthood and religious life* in relation to the whole Body of the Church. Our common pastoral experience confirms the fact that there is *a very special need in the Church today to promote vocations to the priesthood and to religious life....* In every age the Church not only

---

2 Pope Paul VI, *Sanctitatis Clarior*, March 19, 1969. The same point is reiterated by Pope John Paul II: see his homily of May 9, 1988, and *Christifideles Laici*, n. 16.

reiterates her esteem for these vocations but she acknowledges their unique and irreplaceable character.[3]

We will begin this examination of vocation with a consideration of the universal vocation to holiness. For the source and reference point of every vocation is the vocation to baptism and to holiness, the vocation to union with God in Christ. We must therefore first consider this common vocation—the end to which we are called, and the means given us for reaching that end.

After this consideration of the common vocation of all men to holiness, we will turn to consider specific vocations, and the basic ways in which one may seek to discern one's vocation. St. Thomas will be taken as a representative of the first viewpoint, which looks at vocation primarily from the vantage of the good to which man is called, and St. Ignatius of Loyola as a representative of the second viewpoint, which looks at vocation primarily from the vantage of the will of God by which man is called. Following a consideration of each point of view, we will consider vocation as presented by Pope John Paul II, who to some extent unites the two views in a single account, and by Pope Benedict XVI.

Finally, we will turn to a somewhat more practical application of these considerations. First we will point out both the value and the dangers of some of the modern approaches to vocational discernment. Then, on the basis of the preceding considerations of vocation, we will make a proposal for a simple presentation of the issue of vocational discernment and decisions regarding states of life.

---

3   Pope John Paul II, Letter to the Bishops of the Unites States of America, May 14, 1986. See also Pope Paul VI's address to the General Chapters of Religious Orders and Congregations, cited below, on page 49.

Chapter 1: Principles of Christian Life

The goal of Christian life, and indeed of all human life, is union with God, which is realized in this life by charity; for by charity we no longer live our own life, but God lives in us, and we live in God (cf. 1 John 4:16; Eph 3:17; Gal. 2:20). For this reason, our life will be more perfect to the extent that our love is greater. "The greatness of each soul is judged by the measure of love that it has, so that, for instance, he who has great love is great, he who has little love is little, while he who has no love at all is nothing, as St. Paul says: 'If I have not love, I am nothing.'"[1]

We will love God in the fullest way in heaven, when seeing him face to face, our heart will always be actually moved towards him in love, and all that we think and do will be referred to him. This perfect way of loving God is impossible to us in this life; for since we do not see God as he is in himself, our heart is not at every moment animated with love for him, and we are attracted to other good things without consciously referring them to him as their source and exemplar.

But even in this life we can love God perfectly in two ways. First, when everything we love, and everything we do, we refer at least implicitly to God as our end and goal. We will do this if, having chosen God as the ultimate goal of our life, we do not love or choose anything that is incompatible with God's being our last end. For the power of the choice by which we choose God carries over into the further things we do, even when we do not explicitly refer them to God as an end.[2] Perfect love in this sense is required of all. For since God is the perfect good, he who does not love God perfectly in the sense of somehow referring all things to him, does not really love God.

---

1   St. Bernard, *Sermons on the Song of Songs*, 27, n. 10, PL 183:919.
2   See *In II Sent.*, d. 40, q. 1, a. 5, ad 6 & 7; *In IV Sent.*, d. 15, q. 4, a. 2, qa. 4; ST I-II 1:6 ad 3.

2

Secondly, we can possess the perfect love of God in this life in the sense that we are moving towards such a perfect love as we will possess in heaven, i.e., inasmuch as we are always growing in love. This perfection is not absolutely required—it is possible to love God without growing in the love of God. However, the objective tendency of the love of God, who is the infinite good, is such that one either grows in that love, or somehow opposes it, and comes into danger of losing that love altogether. "Not to go forwards in the way of life, is to go backwards."[3] One who does not even wish to grow in the love of God does not meet the demands of love. "All are bound to tend to the perfection [that consists in the love of God and neighbor], since if someone did not want to love God more, he would not be doing what charity demands."[4] Thus growth in the love of God is necessary for the well-being of the love of God, and for its surer preservation.

We will grow in the love of God to the extent that all of our strength is given to this love. "Man stands between the things of this world and spiritual goods, in which eternal happiness consists, so that to the degree he clings more to one of them, so much does he draw back from the other."[5] The reason for this is that we are finite beings, with finite powers. To the extent that we attend to many things and our love is drawn to them, it is less focused on any one of them. St. Thomas explains how emotions can hinder the activity of the will, due to the fact that we are unified beings.

> Every power dispersed among many things becomes less; hence, conversely, when a power is applied intensely to one thing, it can be less dispersed among other things. Moreover, a certain attention is required in the soul's works, so that when it is powerfully focused on one thing, it cannot powerfully attend to another.[6]

---

3 St. Bernard, *Second Sermon for the Feast of the Purification*, PL 183:369; cf. *Epistle* 385, n. 1, PL 182:588; St. Gregory the Great, *Pastoral Rule*, Part III, Admonition 35, PL 77:118.
4 St. Thomas Aquinas, *Commentary on the Letter to the Hebrews*, Ch. 6, Lec. 1.
5 ST I-II 108:4.
6 ST I-II 77:1; cf. ST I-II 37:1, and St. Francis de Sales, *Treatise on the Love of God*, Bk. 5, Ch. 7.

For this reason, to the extent that our love is less dispersed, and is focused more entirely on God, we will be enabled to love God more intensely. And in this way, by a fervent practice of the love of God, our love for God will grow more and more.

Commandments

Christian perfection consists essentially in charity, which unites us to God. "You shall love the Lord your God with all your heart, and with all your soul, and with all your mind. This is the great and first commandment. And a second is like it, You shall love your neighbor as yourself. On these two commandments depend all the law and the prophets" (Mt 22:37–40). The other commandments are for the sake of charity, either prescribing things that are required by charity, as "Honor your father and your mother" (Dt 5:16), or prohibiting things that are incompatible with charity, as "You shall not kill" (Dt 5:17). Because all the other commandments are ordered to charity, St. Paul describes charity as the "fulfilling of the law."

> Owe no one anything, except to love one another; for he who loves his neighbor has fulfilled the law. The commandments, "You shall not commit adultery, You shall not kill, You shall not steal, You shall not covet," and any other commandment, are summed up in this sentence, "You shall love your neighbor as yourself." Love does no wrong to a neighbor; therefore love is the fulfilling of the law (Rom 13:8–10).

So charity is the goal, and the commandments are means to reach this goal. If we do not keep the commandments, we do not truly love God or neighbor, at least not with supernatural love. St. John goes so far as to say, "This *is* the love of God, that we keep his commandments."[7] Moreover, the love of God and of neighbor is included in the commandments insofar as this love is the end of the commandments. Hence our perfection consists essentially in the fulfillment of the commandments and the attainment of their end, which is love.[8] Pope John Paul II notes that since all the commandments are ordered to love, they themselves indicate not

---

7 1 John 5:3 (emphasis added).
8 See ST II-II 184:3, and the *Catechism of the Catholic Church*, n. 1974.

only the conditions we must fulfill, but also the goal for which we are to aim.

> Jesus shows that the commandments cannot be understood as a minimum limit not to be gone beyond, but rather as a path that opens up to a moral and spiritual journey towards perfection, the heart of which is love.[9]

Counsels

In addition to the commandments, we are given the counsels, which are not necessary in order to attain the goal, which is love of God and neighbor, but are means useful for attaining this goal more surely and completely. The Catechism of the Catholic Church, adopting St. Thomas' description of the difference between the commandments and counsels, distinguishes them on the basis of their different relationship to love:

> Besides its precepts, the New Law also includes the evangelical counsels. The traditional distinction between God's precepts and the evangelical counsels is drawn in relation to charity, the perfection of Christian life. The precepts are intended to remove whatever is incompatible with charity. The aim of the counsels is to remove whatever might hinder the development of charity, even if it is not contrary to it.[10]

Now our attention should be turned to God in two ways. First, we should trust in God for all we need, relying on him as a loving Father. All that happens or may happen to us we should see as coming from his loving and wise providence. "It is Christ's hand that guides *everything*. We must see him alone in *everything*."[11] Secondly, we should always make God our last end. All that we do, we should do for the sake of God. "The *littlest things* done out of love are those that charm our Lord's Heart";[12] "Jesus looks neither at the greatness of our actions, nor at their difficulty, but at the love

---

9 Pope John Paul II, *Veritatis Splendor,* n. 15.
10 *Catechism of the Catholic Church,* n. 1973. cf. St. Thomas Aquinas, ST II-II 184:3.
11 St. Thérèse of Lisieux, LT 149, October 20, 1893.
12 St. Thérèse of Lisieux, LT 191, July 12, 1896.

that makes us do these acts."[13] The more consistently we actually place our confidence in God, and actually direct our love to him, not just implicitly, the more surely we will grow in confidence and in love. This practice of actual trust in God and this constant love for him are the goal of the counsels, and may be considered as two universal counsels, which give us the aim for which we are to strive in the practice of the other counsels, just as love is both the end of the other commandments, and is itself commanded inasmuch as we are to strive for love.[14] St. Paul instructs us to "do all things for the glory of God" (1 Cor 10:31). As St. Thomas explains, we can understand this instruction as a precept, to do nothing contrary to God's glory, and to refer everything at least implicitly to God. Or we can understand it a more direct sense: "[It can also be understood to mean], whatever you do, it is better if you actually refer it to God; and in this sense it is a counsel."[15]

The means by which the counsels accomplish this aim are simple: the counsels take away those material and temporal goods that tend to distract or weaken our focus on God, or to make us rely upon such temporal goods. Unlike the commandments, the counsels do not separate us from bad things that are incompatible with love of God. Rather, they separate us from things that are in themselves *good*, even very good, but that are not the greatest good, and thus can hinder a direct focus on the greatest goods, and on the giver of all good things.

The reason why separating ourselves from things that are good is helpful for focusing on the highest good and source of all goods, on God himself, is that as was said above, we are finite beings with finite capacities for attention and love. Therefore, by removing our attention and love from worldly and temporal goods, the counsels help us to fix them more fully on spiritual and eternal

13 St. Thérèse of Lisieux, LT 65, October 20, 1888.
14 The basic lines of this comparison can be found in many sources. See, among others, St. Thomas Aquinas's discussions of the counsels in *Quodlibetal* 4, q. 12, a. 12, and *Quodlibetal* 5, q. 10, a. 1; *Contra Doctrinam Retrahentium*, Ch. 6; Thomas à Kempis, *Imitation of Christ*; Br. Lawrence, *Practice of the Presence of God*; St. Thérèse of Lisieux, autobiography and letters; de Caussade, *Abandonment to Divine Providence.*
15 *In II Sent.*, d. 40, q. 1, a. 5, ad 7.

6

goods, on God himself. St. Thomas describes this well in his work *On the Perfection of the Spiritual Life*:

> It is manifest that the human heart is given over more intensely to one thing to the extent that it is withdrawn from a multiplicity of things. Thus man's mind is given over more perfectly to loving God to the extent that it is removed from love for temporal things... Therefore all the counsels, by which we are invited to perfection, have as their aim the turning away of man's mind from love for temporal things, so that his mind may tend more freely to God, by contemplating, loving, and fulfilling his will.[16]

In the present climate, it is important to emphasize that the counsels are not proposed as good because the things we give up by following the counsels are bad, but because there is a better way to grow in love than the use of these things. Giving up marriage, for example, enables one to grow more in the love of God and neighbor, not because marriage is bad, but because the direct and complete dedication of our heart and mind to God is a better means for growing in love than marriage is, whether considered in itself or as a sacrament.[17] Pope John Paul II beautifully describes this superiority that virginity or celibacy consecrated to God possesses over marriage.

> The reference to the nuptial union of Christ and the Church gives marriage itself its highest dignity: in particular, the sacrament of matrimony makes the spouses enter into the mystery of Christ's union with the Church. However, the profession of virginity or celibacy enables consecrated persons to share more directly in the mystery of this marriage. While conjugal love goes to Christ the Bridegroom through a human union, virginal love goes directly to the person of Christ through an immediate union with him, without intermediaries: a truly complete and decisive spiritual espousal. Thus in the person of those who profess and live consecrated chastity, the Church expresses her union as Bride with Christ the Bridegroom to the greatest extent. For this

---

16 St. Thomas Aquinas, *On the Perfection of the Spiritual Life*, Ch. 7.
17 See *Sacra Virginitas*, by Pope Pius XII, nn. 37–39.

reason it must be said that the virginal life is found at the heart of the Church.[18]

Evangelical Counsels

The three counsels traditionally called evangelical have here a special place. They in a certain way contain all the other counsels within themselves: chastity is the most radical way of putting one's body at the service of the Lord, poverty the most radical way of putting external goods at this service, and obedience the most radical way of putting one's own self at this service, inasmuch as it is by one's will that one possesses and is master of oneself. This traditional understanding is summed up by Pope John Paul II in his encyclical on religious life, *Redemptionis Donum.*

> If, in accordance with Tradition, the profession of the evangelical counsels is *centered on the three points of chastity, poverty and obedience*, this usage seems to emphasize sufficiently clearly their importance as key elements and in a certain sense as a "summing up" of the entire economy of salvation.... "The lust of the flesh, the lust of the eyes and the pride of life" are present deep within man as the *inheritance of original sin*, as a result of which the relationship with the world, created by God and given to man to be ruled by him (cf. Gen 1:28), was disfigured in man's heart in many ways. In the economy of the Redemption the evangelical counsels of chastity, poverty and obedience constitute the most efficacious means for transforming in man's heart this relationship with "the world."...
>
> In the context of these words taken from *the first letter of St. John*, it is easy to see the extreme importance of the three evangelical counsels in the whole economy of Redemption. For *evangelical chastity* helps us to transform in our interior life everything that arises from the lust of the flesh; *evangelical poverty*, everything that is born from the lust of the eyes; and evangelical *obedience* enables us wholly to reform that

---

18 Pope John Paul II, General Audience of November 23, 1994.

8

which in the human heart proceeds from the pride of life.[19]

Devotion to the Lord

The commandments and the counsels are the objective means for attaining holiness—the commandments are necessary means, and the counsels, though not necessary, are better and useful means. Does it then follow that it is always better to follow the counsels? It does not, for two reasons. First, as St. Francis de Sales notes, the counsels are at the service of charity, and charity may sometimes demand that we not follow the counsels.

> God does not want each person to observe all the counsels, but only those that are appropriate to the diversity of persons, times, occasions, and abilities, as charity requires; for it is charity, as queen of all virtues, all commandments, all counsels, and in short, of all laws and all Christian actions, that gives to all of them their rank, order, time, and value.[20]

Secondly, even if one is able to follow a counsel legitimately, i.e., if he is not bound by charity to do something else, it may not be most beneficial for him to embrace that counsel. If he is not going to make use of the counsel for the sake of love, it will be at best a pointless rejection of something good, and at worst an occasion for some vice. Thus St. Thomas says that poverty is beneficial as a means for spiritual freedom, if one uses this freedom well, but it is harmful if it is not used well.

> Insofar as it takes away the anxiety which arises from wealth, poverty is useful for some, namely those who are disposed so as to be occupied with better things, while harmful to those, who, freed from this anxiety, fall into worse occupations.[21]

Similarly one who gives up marriage will not be any better off for doing so, if he does not use the freedom of his heart that not

---

19 Pope John Paul II, *Redemptionis Donum*, Chapter IV, n. 9; see ST II:II 186:7.
20 St. Francis de Sales, *Treatise on the Love of God*, Book 8, Ch. 6.
21 St. Thomas Aquinas, *Summa Contra Gentiles*, Book 3, Ch. 133.

being married gives him, to devote himself more fully to God and to the service of the Church, or to some greater good of this kind. In fact, he will be worse off, since he will lack the great good of marriage as well as the greater good of virginity or celibacy. In his audiences on the theology of the body, Pope John Paul II notes that the single state, if it is not chosen, or at least used for higher purposes, leads not to a dedication of the heart, but to a kind of division of heart—i.e., it makes there be no truly unifying central goal of one's heart and life.

> Paul observes that the man who is bound by the marriage bond "finds himself divided" (1 Cor 7:34) because of his family duties (see 1 Cor 7:34). From this observation, it seems thus to follow that the unmarried person should be characterized by an *inner integration*, by a unification that would allow him to devote himself completely to the service of the kingdom of God in all its dimensions. This attitude presupposes abstention from marriage, exclusively "for the kingdom of God," and a life directed uniquely to this goal. Otherwise "division" can secretly enter also the life of an unmarried person, who, being deprived, on the one hand, of married life and, on the other hand, of a clear goal for which he should renounce marriage, could find himself faced with a certain emptiness.[22]

The intention and purpose with which one embraces the counsels is therefore absolutely essential. Just as one should not enter marriage merely for the sake of money or pleasure, but should seek in marriage the goods proper to marriage, so one who follows the counsels should seek the goods for the sake of which the counsels were given. Accordingly, Pope John Paul II notes the necessity of the proper motivation for embracing the counsel of continence.

> If someone chooses marriage, he must choose it exactly as it was instituted by the Creator "from the beginning"; he must seek in it those values that correspond to the plan of God. If on the other hand someone decides to follow continence for the kingdom of heaven, he must seek in it the values proper to such a vocation. In other

---

22 Pope John Paul II, General Audience, July 7, 1982.

10

words, *he must act in conformity with his chosen vocation.*[23]

Moreover, granting in each case the right intention, the intensity and steadfastness of one's resolve to pursue holiness using the means one chooses is of greater importance than the means that one chooses for oneself. It is better to seek holiness in marriage wholeheartedly, than to seek holiness in religious life halfheartedly. St. Alphonsus goes so far as to say that one who is not ready to serve God wholeheartedly in religious life, should not enter at all.

> A final caution to him who wishes to enter religious life: let him resolve to become holy, and to suffer every exterior and interior pain, in order to be faithful to God, and not to abandon his vocation. And if he is not so resolved, I exhort him not to deceive the superiors and himself, and not to enter; for this is a sign that he is not called, or else what is even worse, that he does not want to respond to the call as he ought. Hence, with so bad a disposition it is better for him to remain outside, in order to dispose himself better, and to resolve to give himself entirely to God, and to suffer all for God.[24]

Karol Wojtyła similarly notes that the difference of means for attaining perfection, i.e., for growing in the love of God, is less important than the attitude one takes towards this pursuit of perfection, i.e., to what extent one is committed to seeking to grow in love.

> According to the consistent teaching and practice of the Church, virginity realized as a deliberately chosen life-vocation, based on a vow of chastity, and in combination with the two other vows of poverty and obedience, creates particularly favorable conditions for attaining evangelical perfection. The combination of conditions that results from applying the evangelical counsels in the lives of particular men, and especially in communal life, is called the state of perfection. The "state of perfection,"

---

23 Pope John Paul II, General Audience, April 21, 1982; see also his General Audience of March 31, 1982.
24 St. Alphonsus Liguori, "Counsels Concerning a Religious Vocation," *Opere Ascetiche*, in *Opere di S. Alfonso Maria de Liguori* vol. 4 (Torino: Marietti, 1880), 411–12.

however, is not the same as perfection itself, which is realized by every man through striving in the manner proper to his vocation to fulfill the commandment to love God and one's neighbor. It may happen that a a man who is outside the "state of perfection," is, by observing this greatest commandment, effectively more perfect than someone who chose that state. In the light of the Gospel, every man solves the problem of his vocation in practice above all by adopting a conscious personal attitude towards the supreme demand contained in the commandment of love. This attitude is above all a function of a person; the state (marriage, celibacy, even virginity understood only as the "state" or an element of the state) plays in it a secondary role.[25]

For this reason, some should not live the religious life, even if they are capable of living it. As St. Paul says, "each has his own gift from God, one of one kind, and another of another" (1 Cor 7:7). Some discover after entering a religious community and living the religious life for a time, that they are incapable of putting their whole heart into it. They usually experience this in some form of unhappiness, dissatisfaction, or lack of inner peace. These things are not, however, always due to a basic incapacity of their heart to give itself to such a way of life. They can also be due to a culpable negligence, a failure to be substantially faithful to the tasks and attitudes required by this way of life. Or again, unhappiness or dissatisfaction can be the result of personal or psychological problems that will surface and be an obstacle to peace in any way of life. Neither religious life nor marriage is an automatic cure for one's psychological problems. Therefore, in such a case, one must discern whether such an experience of not feeling happy, or lacking peace, is due to having made a mistake in one's choice of a state of life, or whether it is due to some personal problem that can be overcome.

On the other hand, pursuing holiness wholeheartedly does not necessarily require that one be attracted to the way of life that one chooses, or that one lack attraction for another way of life. And

25 Karol Wojtyła, *Love and Responsibility*, 2nd edition, translated by H.T. Willetts (San Francisco: Ignatius Press, 1993), Ch. 4, p. 258. The translation was edited to correspond more closely to the Polish text.

indeed, if one puts one's whole heart into pursuing holiness in the religious life despite a lack of attraction to it, one's intention will tend to be even purer and more intense. To her Sister Céline, who plans to enter the Carmelite monastery, St. Thérèse of Lisieux writes as follows:

> I am very happy, my dear little sister, that you do not feel a sensible attraction to come to the Carmel; that is a treat from Jesus, who wants to receive a *gift* from you. He knows that it is much sweeter to give than to receive. We have only the brief moment of our life to *give* to the good God.[26]

St. Teresa of Avila similarly says that God shows great favor to those who give themselves entirely to his service despite their own disinclination.

> Though I did not succeed to incline my will to being a nun, I saw that this was the best and safest state, and so, little by little, I determined to force myself to embrace it....
>
> When I took the habit, the Lord soon made me understand how greatly he favors those who use force with themselves in serving him.[27]

In summary, because we attain the true end of our lives to the extent that we grow in love, the decisive factor in our vocation is our dedication to pursuing constant growth in love. But subordinate to this, and also of significance, are the objective means we choose for pursuing this goal. Given an equal dedication on our part, we will attain the goal more perfectly if we employ means which are in themselves more suited to reaching this goal, as for example, the evangelical counsels.

---

26 St. Thérèse of Lisieux, LT 169, August 19, 1894.
27 St. Teresa of Avila, *Autobiography*, Ch. 3–4.

Chapter 2: Two Approaches to the Question of Vocation

St. Thomas Aquinas

St. Thomas does not often use the term "vocation." However, he speaks in several places about making the choice to enter religious life, which is one particular vocation. In the *Summa Theologiae*, at the very end of the treatise on the states of life, St. Thomas asks the question "whether it is praiseworthy for someone to enter religious life without long deliberation, and having taken counsel from many people."[1] He answers "yes," with the following argument. Long deliberation is required for great and doubtful things, but not for things which are certain and determined. Now we can consider religious life in itself, or we can consider it in relation to an individual's ability to live religious life. Since Christ counseled religious life, it is certain that considered in itself it is better to enter it.[2] And since those who enter religious life look for the ability to live it not from themselves, but from God, there is also no reason in general for doubt concerning one's ability to live that life. If someone has *specific* obstacles, such as bodily weakness, great debts, or similar things, then deliberation is required, and counsel from people who can be expected to help and not to hinder him. St. Thomas notes that even in this case long deliberation is not necessary. He adds that counsel may also be taken as to the manner of entering, and which religious order one should enter.

St. Thomas does not, then, place the idea of vocation at the heart of his consideration. Rather, the primary question is, "Is it good?" St. Thomas puts the question this way not because vocation

---

1 ST II-II 189:10.

2 The term "religious life" does not come from Christ himself, but Christ did establish this form of life, and gave the three counsels of chastity, poverty, and obedience, upon which religious life is based. See Pope John Paul II, *Redemptionis Donum*, n. 3, as well as his General Audience of December 7, 1994.

14

is unimportant, but because it is secondary. A vocation is a means God uses to lead us to something good, so the most important thing is not the vocation itself, but the good to which he wants to lead us. In general, the vocation to holiness is subordinate to holiness; in particular, the vocation to religious life is subordinate to the religious life as a specific way of living the Christian life, and the vocation to marriage is subordinate to marriage as a specific way of living the Christian life.

The idea of vocation, though not the term itself, appears in one of the objections in this article. The claim is made that the desire and will to live the religious life is not always from God, and therefore one needs to examine this desire, to determine whether it is from God.

> It is said, "Do not believe every spirit, but test whether the spirits are from God" (1 John 4:1). But sometimes the will to live the religious life is not from God, since frequently it is dissolved by leaving the religious life. For it is said, "If this plan or work is from God, you will not be able to dissolve it" (Acts 5:39). Therefore it seems that people should enter religious life only after much examination.[3]

St. Thomas' response to this objection is basically that if one's desire is sincere, then since it is for something good, it is certainly from God.

> The saying, "Test whether the spirits are from God," applies to things about which there is some doubt as to whether it is the Spirit of God [that is at work]. Thus those who are in religious life can have doubt as to whether he who offers himself for the religious life is led by the Spirit of God, or is merely pretending. But for him who seeks religious life, there can be no doubt as to whether the will to enter religious life that has arisen in his heart is from the Spirit of God, to whom it belongs to lead man to the right land (cf. Ps 143:10)... And therefore the will to enter religious life does not need to be tested to see whether it is from God; for "things that

---

3   ST II-II 189:10 obj. 1.

are certain do not need discussion," as the Gloss says about the precept, "Test all things" (1 Thess. 5:21).[4]

Similarly in his defense of religious life, St. Thomas writes that there is no reason for doubting whether one's desire to follow the evangelical counsels is from God; for although these counsels were given to particular men, they were intended for all men.

> Our opponents say that the aforesaid certainty has place if someone is called by the words of the Lord himself; for then they admit that one should not delay, nor seek additional advice. But when a man is moved interiorly to enter religious life, then there is need of great deliberation and the advice of many people, so that he can discern whether this movement comes from God.
>
> But this response is quite wrong. For we should take Christ's words written in Sacred Scripture, as though we heard them from the mouth of the Lord himself. For he himself says, "What I say to you, I say to all: be watchful'; and in Romans it is said that "whatever was written, was written for our instruction." And Chrysostom says, "If they had been said only for the sake of those men, they would not have been written; now however they have indeed been said for their sake, but they have been written for our sake."...
>
> Let us see specifically whether the advice that the Lord gave to the young man, "If you wish to be perfect, go and sell all that you have, and give to the poor" (Mt. 19:21), was given to him alone, or also to all. We can find the answer from what follows; for when Peter said to him, "Behold we have left all things and have followed you," he assigns a reward universally for all: "Everyone who leaves house or brothers etc...., for my name's sake, will receive a hundredfold, and will possess eternal life." Therefore this advice should be followed by any particular person no less than if it were given personally to him by the mouth of our Lord himself.[5]

---

4 ST II-II 189:10 ad 1.

5 *Contra Doctrinam Retrahentium*, ch. 9. Some saints have done quite literally what St. Thomas describes here. St. Anthony of the desert, for example, heard in church the words, "If you would be perfect, go sell what you have, etc.," and followed them as though spoken personally to him.

Here too, then, St. Thomas looks at the matter objectively. In other words, he argues that the desire to follow the evangelical counsels is good, and can be immediately carried out, because this desire corresponds to the counsel of Christ, which he gave generally to men as a means for attaining perfection—an objective standard, by which our desires can be measured.

On the other hand, in the very same passage, St. Thomas also speaks of the Holy Spirit speaking interiorly, as contrasted with Christ's advice, which is given to us through Holy Scripture.

> There is also another way in which God speaks interiorly to man, as the Psalm says, "I will hear what the Lord God speaks within me," and this speaking is superior to any external speaking.... Therefore if one should immediately obey the voice of the Creator uttered externally, as they themselves say, much more should no one resist the interior speaking, by which the Holy Spirit moves the mind, but should obey without hesitation. As is said by the mouth of the prophet, or rather of Christ himself, "the Lord God opened an ear to me," namely by inspiring him interiorly, "and I did not contradict, I did not go back," as though "forgetting what lies behind, stretching forward to what lies ahead" (Phil 3:13). The Apostle also says that "they who are led by the Spirit of God are sons of God" (Rom 8:14), on which Augustine's Gloss says, "not because they do nothing, but because they are led by the impulse of grace." But he who resists or delays is not led by the impulse of the Holy Spirit. Therefore it is characteristic of the sons of God to be led by the impulse of grace to better things, without awaiting advice.... The Apostle teaches that this impulse should be followed: "Walk by the Spirit"; and again, "if you are led by the Spirit, you are not under the law."... He also says: "Do not extinguish the Spirit" (1 Thess 5:19), on which the Gloss says, "If the Holy Spirit reveals something to someone at the present moment, do not prevent him from speaking." Now the Holy Spirit reveals not only by teaching what a man should say, but also by suggesting what a man should do, as is said in John 14. Therefore when a man is moved by the impulse of the Spirit to enter religious life, he should not put it

off for the sake of seeking human counsel, but should immediately follow the impulse of the Holy Spirit.[6]

Thus it seems that the fact that a desire to live religious life is in conformity with Christ's objective advice, does not necessarily mean that this desire is from the Holy Spirit.

There are two solutions to this apparent difficulty. First, the movement of the Holy Spirit is distinct from, but not opposed to other motives, such as the fact that Christ advises something in the Scriptures. Indeed, whenever man is enlightened to see spiritual truth, and moved to spiritual good, it is the work of the Holy Spirit. It is ultimately God alone who enlightens one to see the truth, and moves one to love and choose the good. For this reason, St. Thomas concludes that if a man sincerely desires to enter religious life in order to grow in the love of God, he can be confident that this desire is from God.

> The saying which is brought forward in the third place, "Test whether the spirits are from God," does not prove the point. For testing is necessary where there is not certainty; hence on the text "test all things," the Gloss says, "Things that are certain do not need discussion." Now to those who are in a position of accepting others into religious life, there may be doubt about in what spirit these persons come to religious life, namely whether they come out of a desire for spiritual progress, or as is sometimes happens, they come for investigating or evildoing; or there may be doubt about whether those who come are fit for religious life. And therefore a testing of those who are to be received, is appointed both by the Church's ordinance and by the religious rule. But to those who pursue the intention of taking up religious life, there can be no doubt regarding with what intention they do it. Hence no necessity of deliberating lies upon them, especially if they are confident about their bodily strength, for examining which a year of testing is granted to those who enter religious life.[7]

It does not matter whether God is the immediate source of the movement, or employs instruments to draw someone to

---

6   Ibid.
7   Ibid., ch. 10.

18

religious life. Indeed, even if the devil himself were a source of the movement, the movement itself would be for good, and would be ultimately from God.

> What is proposed fourthly, that Satan transforms himself into an angel of light, and many times suggests good things with the intention of deceiving, is true. But as the Gloss on that passage says, "when the devil deceives the bodily sense, but does not move the mind from true and right judgment, by which each one leads a faithful life, there is no danger in religious life; or when pretending to be good, he either does or says those things that are fitting to good angels, even if he is believed to be a good angel, it is not a dangerous or unhealthy error."... Therefore given that the devil incited someone to enter religious life, this would be a good work, and fitting to the good angels. Hence there would not be a danger if someone consented to him in this; but he would have to be watchful to resist him when he began to [try to] lead him to pride or to other vices. For it frequently happens that God uses the malice of demons for the good of the saints... Yet it should be known that if the devil suggests to someone that he enter religious life, or if another man suggests this to him, this suggestion has no efficacy unless he is drawn interiorly by God; for by entering religious life, one sets out to follow Christ, [and no one can come to Christ unless the Father draws him].[8]

The first solution, then, is that one and the same movement may have an origin both in the Holy Spirit, and in the counsels of Christ. In fact, in this sense the movement of the Holy Spirit is an internal element of every true vocation.

There is also another response to this difficulty, namely that there are two different legitimate ways of choosing a way of life. The first way of choosing, which St. Thomas presents as the normal way, consists in making a choice on the basis of a judgment about the way of life itself. In this case, one would judge one's inclination to a way of life, on the basis of a judgment about the value of that way of life and one's fitness for it. Since the way of life is good, and one is fit to live it, one can conclude that the will to live it is from the Holy Spirit. Sometimes, however, one may be

8   Ibid., ch. 10.

able in a certain sense to judge directly that an inclination or movement of the will is from the Holy Spirit, without judging it on the basis of its object. And for this reason St. Thomas distinguishes internal from external calling, as though different instances of vocation.

> It is therefore not praiseworthy, but rather blameworthy, after an internal or external calling, made either in words or in the Scriptures, to put it off and to seek counsel as though about a doubtful matter.[9]

Of course, there is a danger of our thinking that a desire is inspired by the Holy Spirit when it in fact simply arises from our own inclinations. And for this reason a choice made on the basis of such a perceived inspiration should generally be confirmed or backed up by other reasons, such as those based on the objective character and circumstances of that which is chosen.

St. Ignatius of Loyola

According to many of the followers of St. Ignatius of Loyola, the Spiritual Exercises include radical innovations, at least in comparison to the practice of the earlier medieval age. According to P. Everard Mercurian, who later became Superior General of the Society of Jesus, the Spiritual Exercises contain many "unheard of" innovations.

> Our spiritual exercises, in the matter of election, encompass everything that can be found about that matter in all the doctors and saints; indeed many new and unheard of things are proposed there, especially where they concern the threefold time for making a choice.[10]

Hans Urs von Balthasar, an influential twentieth century theologian who was ordained as a Jesuit priest, does not go quite so far as to say "unheard of," but does stress the newness of St. Ignatius' approach at least in comparison with the medieval approach: "The Book of the Exercises by St. Ignatius of Loyola,

---

9 Ibid., ch. 9.

10 *Directoria Exercitiorum Spiritualium, Monumenta Ignatiana*, Series 2, Vol. 2. (Rome: Monumenta Historica Societatis Iesu, 1955), 269 (Hereafter cited as *Directoria*.)

20

looking back to the Gospel, was the first to uncover a new yet decisive dimension, to effect a revolution."[11]

In his explanatory notes to the Spiritual Exercises, St. Ignatius describes what these exercises are: "Every way of preparing and disposing the soul to rid itself of all inordinate attachments, and, after it is rid of them, of seeking and finding the divine will as to the management of one's life for the salvation of one's soul, we call Spiritual Exercises."[12] After removing disordered tendencies, that is, clearing away obstacles to the goal, the positive aspect of the goal is described as "seeking and finding the divine will." In accordance with this aim, he prescribes that the one who is giving the exercises should not, in regard to a state or way of life, influence the one who is making them, but should leave all the action up to God.

> He who is giving the Exercises ought not to urge him who is receiving them more to poverty or to a promise than to their opposites, nor more to one state or way of life than to another. For although outside the Exercises, we can lawfully and meritoriously urge every one who is probably fit, to choose continence, virginity, the religious life, and all manner of evangelical perfection, still in the Spiritual Exercises, in seeking the divine will, it is more fitting and much better that the Creator and Lord Himself should communicate Himself to his devout soul, inflaming it with his love and praise, and disposing it for the way in which it will be better able to serve him in the future. So he who is giving the Exercises should not turn or incline to one side or the other, but standing in the center like a balance, should allow the Creator to act immediately with the creature, and the creature with its Creator and Lord.[13]

St. Ignatius wants to remove from the soul any excessive attachment that would move it to choose one way of life rather than another, whether that be an attachment to selfish inclinations, or an

---

11 Von Balthasar, *Christlicher Stand*, 317.
12 St. Ignatius of Loyola, *Exercitia Spiritualia*, n. 1, *Monumenta Historica Societatis Iesu*, Series 2, Vol. 1 (Rome: Institutum Historicum Societatis Iesu, 1969), 140–42. (This work will be hereafter cited as *Exercitia Spiritualia*.)
13 *Exercitia Spiritualia*, n. 15.

attachment to the opinions of others. This is necessary because a vocation comes from God: "Every divine vocation is always pure and clear, without mixture of flesh, or of any other inordinate attachment."[14] Yet St. Ignatius does not want to remove all preference for one way of life over another, but only all preferences that could be an impediment to the greater service of God, that is, preferences for things that in themselves are less good, which we call "attachments." Indeed, "the greater a good is, the readier we should be to choose it."[15] Consequently, St. Ignatius sees it as most desirable for a person to prefer the way of the counsels, as being more in conformity with Christ's counsels and examples. In his Directory for the Elections he writes:

> It must first of all be insisted that a person entering upon the elections do so with total resignation of will; and if possible, that he reach the third degree of humility, in which for his own part he is more inclined, should it be for the equal service of God, toward that which is most in accord with the counsels and example of Christ our Lord.[16]

While the choice to be made in the spiritual exercises can be any choice that is for the *greater* glory of God, the primary intention of the exercises as a whole is to make the choice of a state of life. Thus in the third time of making a choice, St. Ignatius speaks of choosing "a life or state."[17] And in his Directory for the exercises, he describes the order of making choices in the following manner, clearly expecting that the choice to be made would usually be the choice of a state or way of life:

> The matter proposed for deliberation is: first, whether the counsels or the commandments; secondly, if the counsels, then whether inside or outside a religious institute; thirdly, if in a religious institute, which one; fourthly, after that, when and how. If it is the

---

14 *Exercitia Spiritualia*, n. 172.
15 St. Ignatius of Loyola, Letter 131, in *Letters of St. Ignatius of Loyola*, translated by William J. Young, S.J. (Chicago: Loyola University Press, 1959), 98.
16 Directoria Ignatiana Autographa, n. 17, *Directoria*, pp. 74–76.
17 *Exercitia Spiritualia*, n. 177.

commandments, then in what station or manner of life, etc.[18]

St. Ignatius gives three "times" in which one may choose a state of life. The first depends entirely on God's movement. "The first time is when God our Lord so moves and attracts the will that without doubting, or being able to doubt, the devout soul follows what is shown it, as St. Paul and St. Matthew did in following Christ our Lord."[19]

The second time when one may make a choice of a state of life is when one's spiritual experience is sufficient to form a judgment, "when one gets enough light and knowledge by experience of consolations and desolations, and by the experience of the discernment of various spirits."[20] The basis of judgment in this second time is not directly the objective character of the choice in question, but the causes inclining us to the choice.

The third time when one may make a choice is when one deliberates about what means will best help him to achieve the goal of the glory of God and the salvation of his soul. "The third time is quiet, when one considers, first, for what purpose man is born—namely, to praise God our Lord and to save his soul—and desiring this, chooses as a means to this end, a life or state within the limits of the Church, in order that he may be helped in the service of his Lord and the salvation of his soul."[21]

In this third time there are two ways of making a choice. The first way consists in first putting oneself in an attitude of indifference, and then setting out all of the advantages and disadvantages involved in the choice, and deciding by reason whether the choice furthers the end, namely "to praise God our Lord" and save one's soul.[22]

The second way consists in taking the psychological means that will allow one to make a true and objective judgment about the matter, rather than a judgment influenced by emotion or self-love. First, the desire for the thing should arise out of love for God. "That love which moves me and makes me choose such a thing

---

18 Directoria Ignatiana Autographa, n. 22, *Directoria,* pp. 76–78.
19 *Exercitia Spiritualia,* n. 175.
20 Ibid., n. 176.
21 Ibid., n. 177.
22 Ibid., n. 175.

should descend from above, from the love of God, in such a manner that he who chooses feels first in himself that that love, more or less, which he has for the thing which he chooses, is only for his Creator and Lord."[23] (The purpose of this rule is to remove the influence of self-love.) Secondly, we should choose for ourselves the same thing we would advise someone else in the same circumstances to choose. (The purpose of this rule is to keep us from being influenced by our personal attachments.) Third and fourth, we should choose now that which we would prefer to have chosen when we die, and on the Day of Judgment. (The purpose of these rules is to help us judge according to the ultimate value of the choice, and not its immediate attraction.)[24]

Discernment of spirits

Let us now consider in more detail the second time presented by St. Ignatius, which relies upon the experience of consolation and desolation, and the discernment of various spirits. Some thoughts and desires come from ourselves, some from God, and some from the demons. "I presuppose that there are three kinds of thoughts in me, namely: one which is my own, which springs from my mere liberty and will; and two others, which come from without, one from the good spirit, and the other from the bad."[25]

The movements that arise from God can be discerned by their origin, by their nature, and by their effects. They can be discerned by their origin, because God alone can work immediately in the soul.[26] St. Ignatius explains this characteristic of the divine activity in the soul:

> It belongs to God our Lord alone to give consolation to the soul without any preceding cause, for it is the property of the Creator to enter, go out, and cause movements in the soul, bringing it all into love of his Divine Majesty. I say without cause, that is, without any previous perception or knowledge of any object through

---

23 *Exercitia Spiritualia*, n. 184.
24 Ibid., nn. 185–87.
25 *Exercitia Spiritualia*, n. 32.
26 Cf. ST I 111:2.

which such consolation would come, through one's acts of understanding and will.[27]

They can be discerned by their nature, since these movements are good. "It is proper to God and to his Angels in their movements to give true gladness and spiritual joy, taking away all sadness and disturbance which the enemy causes."[28] On the other hand, to the enemy "it is proper to fight against such spiritual gladness and consolation, bringing apparent reasons, subtleties and continual deceptions."[29]

They can be discerned by their effects, since God works in us for our good, whereas the demons work in us for our harm. If a movement ultimately leads us to something good, it is a sign that it is from God; on the other hand, if it leads us to something bad, or to something less good than the good which we previously intended or possessed, it is a sign that it is from the devil. St. Ignatius explains:

> We ought to note well the course of our thoughts, and if the beginning, middle and end is all good, inclined to all good, it is a sign of the good Angel; but if in the course of the thoughts which he brings it ends in something bad, of a distracting tendency, or less good than what the soul had previously proposed to do, or if it weakens or disquiets or disturbs the soul, taking away the peace, tranquility and quiet which it had before, it is a clear sign that it proceeds from the evil spirit, enemy of our progress and eternal salvation.[30]

There is of course the possibility of deception with regard to any of these signs. The cause of our feeling of joy may be hidden from us, and so we may believe that it must come from God, though it in fact arises from our own dispositions. Emotional excitement, or pride in a new undertaking may be taken for spiritual joy. And because the nature of certain feelings may be hidden from us, we may fail to perceive the evil to which they are tending. For example, a married woman may be led into a harmful and dangerous friendship with a man through a basically sincere

27 *Exercitia Spiritualia*, n. 330.
28 Ibid., n. 329.
29 Ibid.
30 Ibid., n. 333.

belief that her pleasure in his company is due to purely spiritual motives (as may in fact be true in the beginning).

Summary and comparison of the Three Times

The three times when one may make a decision for a state of life, can be briefly described as follows (1): when one has an immediate experience about which there can be no doubt as to its divine source, and which directs one to a state of life; (2) when by much experience and discernment of the working of the Holy Spirit, one perceives that the Spirit by its movement is inviting or pointing one to a state of life, or that the desire for a state of life originates from the Holy Spirit; (3) when, beginning from an attitude of detachment to all created goods, and if possible, with a preference for what in general conforms more to God's will, one makes a prudent choice of a state of life as a means of serving God and saving one's soul.

In the first two times, the choice of a state of life is based on the perception of God's movement or inspiration of the will. In the third time, on the other hand, the choice is based on the usefulness of the means for attaining the end, namely the glory of God and the salvation of our soul, or on other similar comparisons —e.g., comparisons between one's love for God and one's love for the means, or between oneself and someone else whom one would advise.

The first two times of choosing a state of life, when one perceives that one's inclination is from the Holy Spirit, and *thereby* makes a judgment on the goodness of the object of the inclination, seems to be what St. Thomas has in mind when he speaks of the internal vocation effected through the Holy Spirit, not merely as the internal element of every true vocation, but as a distinct instance of vocation. (See above, p. 16 ff.) The third time, when one weighs by reason the advantages of a way or state of life, corresponds with the way St. Thomas generally considers the question of choosing a state of life, inasmuch as it proceeds by means of an objective judgment of the matter.

Because the way of making a choice in the first two times depends more immediately upon God's action, it is considered to be in itself a better way of choosing. Accordingly, St. Ignatius says: "*If* election is not made in the first or the second time, there follow two ways for making it in this third."[31]

On the other hand, because of the possibilities for deception noted above, the second time is a more dangerous way of deciding, while the third time is "usually safer."[32] And in his own directory, St. Ignatius says that one should proceed to the third time not only if no choice is made in the second time, but also if a choice *is* made in the second time, yet does not seem to be a good choice.

> When no decision has been reached in the second mode, or one that is not good in the opinion of the one giving the Exercises (whose task it is to help discern the effects of the good and evil spirit), then the third manner should be resorted to—that of the discursive intellect by means of the six points.[33]

These two points, namely the superiority of the first two times, and the greater security of the third, are summed up in the officially approved directory for the Exercises.

> During the first and second times of election it is the will that takes the lead, with the intellect following and being led by the will, without any reasoning of its own or hesitation. In the third time, on the other hand, the intellect takes the lead, proposing numerous reasons to the will in order to arouse and impel it to the side it judges to be better. And granted that the movement comes directly from God, there is no doubt that the higher and more excellent way is when it is the will which, under God's illumination, takes the lead and draws the intellect after it... On the other hand, the third way by means of reflection and reasoning is safer and more secure.[34]

---

31 Ibid., n. 178 (emphasis added).
32 Annotationes P. Dávila, *Directoria*, 518; see also the Directorium de Polanco, ibid., 314–16; Directoria P. Miró, ibid., 401–2; Vermeersch, *De Religiosis Institutis et Personis*, vol. 1, nn. 124 & 128; Fr. John Hardon, *All My Liberty*, Ch. 7.
33 Directoria Ignatiana Autographa, *Directoria*, 76.
34 Directorium Definitive Approbatum, n. 190, *Directoria*, 701.

Because the third way is a surer way, it is advised as a way of confirming a choice made in the second way. The official directory recommends this as the usual course.

> These two methods that mark the third time, are to be employed not only when no conclusion has been reached in the second time; but also when a choice has been made, the third time contributes to strengthen and confirm it. For if the soul were certain that the movement of the second time were from God, then without doubt it would have no need to look any further. But since the angel of Satan sometimes transforms himself into an angel of light (2 Cor 11:14), this should be the general rule, that it is very dangerous, when a man wishes to govern himself only by movements of the will, and certain inner feelings, without adding appropriate consideration. And therefore there should be a testing and examination by means of the light; for as the Apostle says, "all that is made manifest, is light." Now this light, after the light of faith, is also human reason itself (helped and enlightened, of course, by the light of faith), which is itself from God, and one cannot contradict the other, since truth is necessarily consistent with truth.[35]

In other words, we should not proceed heedlessly, even when led by feelings of devotion, but should reflect upon what we choose to do, in order to avoid being deceived by feelings that are apparently good, but ultimately misleading.

---

35 Directorium Definitive Approbatum, n. 203, *Directoria,* 707–8; cf. Annotationes P. Dávila, nn. 134–35; *Directoria*, 519–20.

Chapter 3: Comparison of the Two Approaches

In the previous chapter we examined two different ways of approaching the question of vocation, namely the objective way taken by St. Thomas, which is based on the goal of vocation, and the more subjective or personal way taken by St. Ignatius Loyola, which is based on the source of vocation. In this chapter we will compare these two approaches, noting both the advantages, and the possible disadvantages or dangers of each approach.

Advantages of the objective approach

St. Thomas' approach to vocation has two significant advantages. First, it is more objective, having as its point of departure the objective evaluation of that which is to be chosen, and the factual condition and circumstances of the one who is making a choice. Due to this objectivity, one is less easily misled. When "the will precedes, and the intellect follows," as happens in the first two times of choosing presented by St. Ignatius, there is a danger of one's inclination not corresponding to the truth. And since our judgment about what is good is affected by our inclinations,[1] this disordered or excessive inclination can lead to a false judgment about what is good. For this reason the official directory lays down the rule that the one to make a choice of a way of life should not have any attachment for an objectively less perfect way.

> If it is perceived that he is inclined too much to wealth, and less to poverty, he would not be well disposed, nor would there be hope of a good outcome in the choice. For that affection which turns away from the more perfect way, and turns toward the less perfect, would move the intellect to come up with reasons corresponding to such an affection. And since, as the saying goes, whatever is received is received according

---

1   ST I-II 9:2.

to the manner of the receiver, it could easily happen that
he would judge to be the will of God, what is in fact his
own will.[2]

On account of this it is recommended that one not begin the
time of decision in the spiritual exercises unless one possesses such
indifference,[3] lest one make a poor choice, and believe it to be the
will of God. A good and wise spiritual director can be a safeguard
against these dangers, and it is for this reason that St. Ignatius urges
constant communication between the one making the exercises and
the one giving them.[4] Unfortunately, many persons are unable to
find such a wise spiritual director.

The objection could be made that in matters such as these
one should not be objective, since the relationship between God
and a human person, where a vocation takes place, is a personal
matter, not an objective one. But this objection overlooks the fact
that a person is characterized by his ability to attain objective truth,
and to order himself to it. If a love-relationship is to be truly
personal, it must also be objective, in the sense of corresponding to
the truth of the persons and matters involved. God speaks to the
human heart, and seeks a response from it; but he speaks to it *as* a
human heart (which implies a heart that is meant to relate to
objective good), and seeks a corresponding response.

Secondly, as regards the vocation that in itself is the higher
vocation, namely the vocation to follow the evangelical counsels,
this approach more easily gives one certainty.[5] It is not difficult to
see why this is so. Since it is based on an objective evaluation, one
does not need a special combination of factors in order to judge that
following the counsels is the better thing to do. Since in themselves
they are objectively better, one would need a special reason to say

---

2   Directorium Definitive Approbatum, n. 171, *Directoria,* 689.

3   Directoria Ignatiana Autographa, nn. 7 & 17, *Directoria,* 70 & 74–76;
Directorium Definitive Approbatum, nn. 171 & 173, *Directoria,* 689 &
691–93.

4   Directoria Ignatiana Autographa, nn. 5 & 19, *Directoria,* 70 & 76;
Directory dictated to Vitoria, n. 11, *Directoria,* 96; Directorium Definitive
Approbatum, nn. 52 & 55, *Directoria,* 601 & 603.

5   For a more extensive treatment of this issue, see Fr. Richard Butler's book
on religious vocation: *Religious Vocation: An Unnecessary Mystery*
(Rockford: Tan Books, 2005).

that following them is *not* the better thing to do. St. Thomas explains:

> In things which are certain and determinate, counsel is not required... It is certain that in itself entering religious life is the better good.... Nevertheless if there is some *specific* impediment, such as bodily weakness or the burden of debts, or something similar, then deliberation is required, and counsel with those whom one hopes will help and not hinder one.[6]

With the other approach, however, which is based on the personal will of God, one seems to need a special reason to say that it is God's will for one to choose this way of life. Simply the fact that it is better is not a good reason to do so. Thus in contrast to the usual way of explaining the evangelical counsels as being proposed to man's free choice,[7] von Balthasar, basing himself on the fact that a lover seeks most of all to do the will of his beloved, argues that one who loves God may not simply choose the way of the counsels, but will have to look first for God's will.

> Love does not impose itself and its self-giving on the beloved; it asks for the will and wish of the beloved, which determine the measure of its self-giving... The beloved alone determines, he only makes the choice of what one may give him... True love is ready to go each way, the harder or the easier way. It is ready to go the way of the commandments, or that of the counsels.[8]

He insists strongly that one may not "anticipate" God's choice, by entering into the way of the counsels, but must wait until God speaks his will.

> While the universal call to perfect Christian love goes out to all, the vocation to the external "state of perfection" is entirely based on the will of God, which chooses one for that state. The distinction of the states that the Lord makes, is determined so much by his choice, that even such as offer themselves to him to be

6 ST II-II 189:10 (emphasis added).
7 St. Basil, *Epistola* 173, PG 32, 647; St. John Chrysostom, *Homilies on Matthew*, 62 & 63, PG 58, 600 & 605; Pope Pius XI, *Casti Connubii*, n.8, AAS 22 (1930), 542.
8 Von Balthasar, *Christlicher Stand*, 42.

his disciples, who believe themselves ready to follow him wherever he gives, he can turn away and send back into the secular state....

Indifference, as readiness for every manifestation of the divine will, is the expression of a love than which—before the Lord has declared his choice—no love could be thought more perfect. Such indifference, and not an anticipation of God's choice by an autonomous entering upon the way of the vows, is the best possible attitude at this stage.[9]

This position, that one needs a special reason to say that it is God's personal will for one to embrace religious life, is a somewhat natural conclusion of this way of approaching the issue. Nevertheless it is not a necessary conclusion, and in fact does not seem to be wholly in accord with St. Ignatius' own understanding. St. Ignatius himself says that fewer signs of God's will are required in order to embrace religious life than to marry: "Greater signs from God are needed for the commandments than for the counsels, inasmuch as Christ our Lord advises the counsels and points out the difficulty in the ownership of property that is possible in the commandments."[10] Again, he says that outside the Spiritual Exercises "we may lawfully and meritoriously urge every one who is probably fit, to choose continence, virginity, the religious life, and all manner of evangelical perfection."[11]

The reason why it is not necessary to have special signs of God's will, is that there exist not only special, but also general indicators of God's will. Thus Christ's counsels are general signs of his will for us. And so, if someone is wholly indifferent, and relies solely upon God's will, he will follow the counsels, unless there are particular reasons not to follow them. In his *Treatise on the Love of God*, St. Francis de Sales describes how the indifferent heart is inclined to the counsels:

Indifference goes beyond resignation: for it loves nothing except for the love of God's will... The indifferent heart is as a ball of wax in the hands of its God, ready to receive equally all the impressions of the

---

9 Ibid., 130–31.
10 Directoria Ignatiana Autographa, n. 9, Directoria, 72.
11 *Exercitia Spiritualia*, n. 15.

eternal good-pleasure; it is a heart without choice, equally disposed for everything, having no other object of its will than the will of its God, and it does not place its love in the things that God wills, but in the will of God who wills them. For this reason, when God's will is in several things, it chooses, at any cost, that thing in which it is most of all. God's good-pleasure is for marriage and in virginity, but because it is more in virginity, the indifferent heart makes choice of virginity though this must cost it its life, as with St. Paul's dear spiritual daughter St. Thecla, with St. Cecily, St. Agatha, and a thousand others. God's will is for the service of the poor and of the rich, but yet somewhat more in serving the poor; the indifferent heart will choose that side. God's will is in moderation practiced among consolations, and in patience among tribulations: the indifferent heart prefers the latter, as having more of God's will in it.[12]

Since there are such general signs of God's will, it does not necessarily follow, from the fact that one wants signs of God's will, that one should seek *special* signs. St. Alphonsus seems to take the same general position as von Balthasar regarding the necessity of signs of God's will. "Regarding the state to be chosen by an adolescent, let the confessor not presume to determine it for him; but from the signs of his vocation, let him take care to recommend to him that state to which he [the confessor] can prudently judge that he is called by God."[13] However, St. Alphonsus does not require special signs of God's will for the one who desires to embrace religious life. In his account, two signs are required, which correspond to what St. Thomas requires: a good and firm intention, and the lack of impediments.

Let the confessor test well the vocation of his penitent, asking whether the penitent has some obstacle to it, due to incapacity, poor health, or the need of his parents. And let him especially weigh his purpose, to see if it is right, i.e., in order to unite himself more closely to God, or to amend the falls of his previous life, or to avoid the

12 St. Francis de Sales, *Treatise on the Love of God*, Book 9, Ch. 4.
13 St. Alphonsus, Praxis Confessarii, Ch. 7, n. 92, in *Theologia Moralis*, Vol. 4, 578.

dangers of the world. But if the primary end is worldly
—in order to lead a more agreeable life, or to free
himself from relatives of an unfeeling character, or to
please his parents, who push him to this—let him beware
of permitting him to enter religious life. For in that case,
it is not a true vocation, and entering in this way, without
a true vocation, will have a bad outcome. But if the end
is good, and no obstacle is present, then neither the
confessor, nor anyone else, as St. Thomas teaches
(Quodlib. 3, art. 14), should or can without grave fault
impede him, or attempt to dissuade him from the
vocation.[14]

Here St. Alphonsus is considering the signs from the point
of view of the confessor, who is in the position of advising a youth.
But on the basis of the same signs, he says that a youth himself can
judge that he has a vocation.

There is a true vocation whenever the following three
things concur. First, a good end, namely, to get away
from the dangers of the world, the better to insure eternal
salvation, and to unite oneself more closely to God.
Secondly, that there is no positive impediment due to
poor health, lack of talents, or some necessity on the part
of one's parents, in regard to which matters the subject
ought to quiet himself by leaving all to the judgment of
the superiors, after having exposed the truth clearly.
Thirdly, that the superiors admit him. Now, whenever
these three conditions are truly present, the novice ought
not to doubt that his vocation was a true one.[15]

St. Alphonsus here adds a third condition for a true
vocation, namely the acceptance by superiors. This official
approval is an important aspect of vocation, especially vocation to
the consecrated life or to the priesthood. God does not call us to
holiness simply as individuals, but as members of the Church, the
Mystical Body of Christ. And for this reason, it is the task of the
Church to test and to ratify a vocation. Someone may feel called to
the priesthood, yet not be accepted by the Church for this sacred

---

14 Ibid., 578–79.
15 St. Alphonsus de Liguori, "Conforto a' novizi per la perseveranza nella
loro vocazione," *Opere Ascetiche*, in *Opere di S. Alfonso Maria de
Liguori*, Vol. 4 (Torino: Marietti, 1880), 439.

position, because of his state or condition—e.g., because he is married, or because he suffers from serious psychological problems. Generally, such a person should humbly accept his situation and this decision of the Church as the will of God. Far from being a rejection of God's inspiration, this humble obedience to the Church is a sign that his desire was from God, while a refusal to obey would be a sign that his desire was not inspired by God. "When God puts inspirations into a heart, the first he gives is obedience.... Whosoever says he is inspired, and yet refuses to obey his superiors and follow their advice, is an impostor."[16] It is in fact sometimes good and right to persevere in the face of opposition from Church officials, and it can be hard to draw the line between this kind of perseverance and simple disobedience. Yet as a matter of principle, it is important for us to distinguish between a laudable perseverance in the face of opposition, and a wrongful disobedience. To discuss this distinction in detail would take us well beyond the scope of this little work on vocation. But in the end, we must remain obedient to the Church, whatever our vocation may be.

Approval by the Church is not as essential for the vocation to marriage as for the vocation to the consecrated life or the priesthood. Yet also in the vocation to marriage, one must be obedient to the Church. If the Church does not permit a marriage between a certain man and woman, for example, that means that they are not called to that marriage, however they may feel about it. And again, once one has entered into marriage, it is necessary to follow the directives and guidelines of the Church in regard to marriage and the upbringing of children.

Though this ratification of a vocation by the Church is very important, it usually comes as a kind of completion of a vocation, rather than at the beginning of it. Just as it would be unusual for a woman to give her consent to marry a man before he expresses his love for her, so it would be unusual for superiors to give their approval to a vocation before a person actually seeks admission to a religious community or to a seminary. In a few cases it is clear that the Church cannot or will not give its approval, as in the case of a man baptized and raised Roman Catholic, who is validly

16 St. Francis de Sales, *Treatise on the Love of God*, Book 8, Ch. 13.

married, and now desires to be a priest. But in most cases, one first makes a personal discernment and decision regarding vocation, and then seeks approval from the Church. And for this reason, though one should always keep the precepts and directives of the Church in mind, it is the first two elements listed by St. Alphonsus that are most relevant for someone who is seeking his vocation: his heart's purpose or resolve, and his freedom from impediments.

If to the second condition mentioned by St. Alphonsus, that one be free from impediments, we add that one have whatever positive qualities are needed to make one fit for the way of life, then we have the conditions that the Church gives both as the requirements for entering religious life, and as the signs of vocation to it. Pope Pius XI writes that a priestly vocation is manifested by the combination of a right intention together with the qualities that make someone suited for the priesthood.

> This readiness to carry out the sacred duties, [i.e., a vocation] is, as you well know, Venerable Brothers, not established so much by some inner inducement of conscience and sensible feeling, which may sometimes be absent, but rather by the right aim and intention in those who desire the priesthood, joined to those physical qualities and spiritual virtues, which make them suitable for embracing this state of life.[17]

This same point is repeated later by the Congregation for Institutes of Consecrated Life and Societies of Apostolic Life, in an instruction on the selection and training of candidates for consecrated life.

> In the free acceptance of this counsel [to the religious life] there is discerned the special call from God or the movement of the Holy Spirit, who interiorly enlightens and inspires a person, who has the other qualifications, to pursue the evangelical counsels or to embrace the priesthood. For the divine inspiration required by St. Pius X in a true vocation,[18] or that marked attraction for

---

17 Pope Pius XI, *Ad Catholici Sacerdotii*, n. 70, AAS 28 (1936), 40. See also the declaration of the Holy See in regard to the Lahitton's work *La Vocation Sacerdotale*, AAS 4 (1912), 485.

18 St. Pius X, Apostolic letter, *Cum primum*, 4 Aug., 1913, in AAS, 5 (1913)–388; Ench. de Stat. Perf., n. 279, p. 331.

sacred duties mentioned by Pius XI in his encyclical letter, Ad Catholici Sacerdotii,[19] is discerned in their right propensity and intention of mind or the choice of their free will (cf. can. 538),[20] rather than in an inner urging of conscience and sensible attraction which may be lacking.[21]

As this point tends to be overlooked or misunderstood, it bears some emphasizing. These conditions are not merely legal requirements for being accepted into religious life, but are authentic signs of the vocation itself—in a certain sense they even constitute the vocation (insofar as they are the things by which God manifests his will and leads someone to a particular state in life). And of these elements, it is the firm will and intention to live a particular state of life (assuming that the choice is legitimate and good in itself) which pertains most properly to the divine vocation. St. Francis de Sales even says that such a firm will *is* a vocation.

> A true vocation is nothing other than the firm and constant will possessed by the person called, to want to serve God in the manner and in the place where the Divine Majesty calls her. This is the best mark one could have to know when a vocation is true.[22]

This firm will should not be confused with a *feeling* of wanting to continue pursuing a path; it is rather the voluntary resolve to do so.

> When I say "a firm and constant will to serve God," I do not mean that from the very beginning she would do everything that is necessary in her vocation with such a firmness and constancy of will that she is free of all repugnance, difficulty or distaste in what depends upon

---

19 Pius XI, Encyc. *Ad Catholici Sacerdotii*, AAS 28, (1936)–39; Ench. de Stat. Perf., n. 367, p. 510.

20 In the 1917 Code of Canon Law—the corresponding canon in the 1983 code is canon 597. (Ed.)

21 *Religiosorum Institutio*, Instruction on the Careful Selection And Training Of Candidates For The States Of Perfection And Sacred Orders, Sacred Congregation for Institutes of Consecrated Life, February 2, 1961, in Canon Law Digest, Bouscaren & O'Connor, Volume 5, Milwaukee, Bruce Publishing Company, 1963, n. 22, p. 465.

22 St. Francis de Sales, "Les vrays entretiens spirituels," Entr. 16; *Œuvres de S. François de Sales*, Vol. 6, 312.

her.... Every human person is subject to such passions, changes, and ups and downs.... We must not judge the firmness and constancy of the will for a good that was earlier embraced, on the basis of such emotions and feelings. But we must consider whether among the variety of different feelings the will remains firm to the point of not leaving behind the good that it has embraced. Even if she feels disgusted or very cold in her love for any virtue, she doesn't on that account stop using the means that are laid down for her to acquire it. So to have the mark of a true vocation, it need not be a sensible constancy, but one that is in the highest part of the spirit, one such as produces effects.[23]

St. Francis de Sales makes the point repeatedly: for a true vocation, what is necessary is not a multitude of virtues, or a disposition to practices of devotion, but a resolution to work perseveringly towards perfection.

We need not expect that those who enter religious life will be immediately perfect; it is enough for them to tend to perfection, and to embrace the means for growing in perfection. And in order to do this, it is necessary to have this firm and constant will such as I spoke of, to embrace all the means of growing in perfection that are proper to the vocation in which one is called.... If you see that she has this constant will of wanting to serve God and to grow in perfection, you may give her your vote; for if she is willing to receive the helps that our Lord will infallibly give her, she will persevere.... Consider a daughter who has strong passions; she is quick-tempered, she commits many faults; if together with this, she really wants to be healed, and wants people to correct her, mortify her, and give her the proper remedies for her healing, however much taking these things causes her anger and difficulty, you must not refuse her your vote.[24]

---

23 Ibid., 312–13.
24 Ibid., 322, 323, 326.

Potential disadvantage of the objective approach—marriage as a vocation

Does this approach to the choice of a state of life allow for marriage as a vocation? On first consideration, it might seem that it does not. For objectively, the consecrated state is the higher state. St. Thomas compares the way of religious life to the other ways as specific to common, inasmuch as the religious life employs special means by which better to attain perfection. "There are two ways of proceeding in the active life: the common way, by means of the commandments; and a specific way, by means of the counsels."[25] Thus a way such as marriage seems simply to coincide with the Christian way itself, which is aimed at the love of God and neighbor, and guided by the commandments. St. Thomas compares this way of life to religious life as the general way to a more specific and better way.

> The commandments taken absolutely, stand to the observance of the commandments with the counsels and the observance of the commandments without the counsels, as a genus to species, just as not-committing adultery stands to not-committing adultery in virginity and not-committing adultery in marriage; and *going* is common to going by horse and going on foot.[26]

Thus there does not seem to be a vocation to marriage, as in any way above and beyond, or specifying the general Christian vocation—it is simply possible to live the Christian vocation in marriage. And consistently with this view, St. Thomas does not speak of a vocation to marriage, but only of vocation to conversion or grace (the usual sense in which he speaks of vocation),[27] and vocation to the more perfect following of Christ by means of the evangelical counsels.[28]

---

25 St. Thomas Aquinas, *In Psalmos*, part 24, n. 4.
26 *Quodlibetale* 5, q. 10, a. 1.
27 See, for example, *In I Sent*. d. 41, q. 1, a. 2, ad 3; *In IV Sent*. d. 17, q. 1, a. 1, qa. 2; *De Veritate* 6:1; *Super Ep. Ad Romanos*, Cap. 8, Lec. 6; Cap. 11, Lec. 4; *Super Evangelium Johannis*, Cap. 1, Lec. 6; Cap. 20, Lec. 3; *Super ad Galatas*, Cap. 1, Lec. 4.
28 Besides the texts where St. Thomas treats of Christ's calling of the disciples: ST II-II 189:10; *Contra Doctrinam Retrahentium*, Ch. 9; *Contra Impugnantes*, Part 2, Ch. 6, ad 13.

Before pursuing this point, we should note that the difficulty does not really arise from taking as one's point of departure the objective character and value of the ways of life rather than the will of God, but from taking seriously the superiority of the religious state as a better means of conforming oneself to Christ, and attaining perfection in love. If God's will and call for all of us is our sanctification and perfection, does he not specially favor and call those whom he calls to the religious state, and therefore is this not a "vocation" in a special sense? Von Balthasar, who continually emphasizes that the distinction of states, both in general and for any particular person, has its origin in God's will, goes so far as to describe the vocation to marriage or the lay-vocation as a "not-being-called" to the evangelical state.

> The call to the state of election is a qualified, special, differentiated call, to which no equally qualified call to the secular state corresponds; rather, in comparison with the state of election, the secular state is distinguished by a not-being-called in this qualified sense.
>
> ... Because it is the instituting will of the Church's founder that the state of those who are called out remain a continual minority in comparison with the common state of believers in the world, it is therefore equally his instituting will that the many who are not called to this special state remain in the common secular state. This instituting will, which does not allow one to consider the secular state as a mere negation of the state of election, but makes it into a real state in the realm of salvation and of the church, cannot, however, be construed as a second call of the Lord that is of equal rank with the first. Being placed in the secular state can only be described as a not-being-called to a qualitatively superior mission.[29]

Pope John Paul II also distinguishes the sense in which there is a vocation to the religious state from the sense in which there is a vocation to marriage. Men and women are naturally ordered to marriage, and in this sense need no special vocation by which they are called to marriage, whereas they are not naturally

---

29 Von Balthasar, *Christlicher Stand*, 116 & 133.

ordered to the state of consecrated celibacy or virginity, and so need a special grace or calling to embrace this state.[30]

> A man and a woman leave their father and mother and join themselves to their own husband or wife to begin a new family (cf. Gn 2:24). The Book of Genesis presents this *vocation of the human creature* in the simplest but very significant words. At a certain moment in life, the young person, male or female, perceives this call and becomes aware of it. Of course, it is a different call from a priestly or religious vocation, for which a special invitation on Christ's part, a personal call to follow him is decisive: "Follow me!" (Mt 4:19)[31]

Let us now consider the question more precisely from St. Thomas' point of view. The goal of Christian life is love for God and neighbor. How does this goal relate to vocation? A vocation, or call, is that by which God leads us somewhere. "Vocation or calling implies a certain leading to something."[32] There is "a certain calling into existence through creation."[33] But most properly, God calls us when he leads us to himself. "There is a temporal calling to grace."[34] Now there are various means, both external and internal, by which God leads us to himself. "This calling is either interior, by means of the influx of grace, or is exterior, by means of a preacher's words."[35] St. Thomas here speaks of vocation insofar as it is that whereby God leads us to grace and to love. Corresponding to this, we can also call grace and love a vocation, or say that we are called to grace and love, insofar as God leads us to it.

There are two ways in which this sense of vocation is extended in regard to states of life: first, when we say that a state of

---

30 The state of celibacy can be chosen for natural motivations. A philosopher might choose this state for the sake of pursuing truth, or a doctor for the sake of his patients. The choice of celibacy for reasons like this can be justified, and even praiseworthy. (See *SCG* 3, n. 136; Karol Wojtyła, *Love and Responsibility*, 256) However, the state of celibacy embraced for such motivations is not yet the evangelical celibacy or virginity that pertains to the consecrated state.

31 Pope John Paul II, Homily of December 15, 1994.

32 *In I Sent*. d. 41, q. 1, a. 2, ad 3.

33 Ibid.

34 Ibid.

35 Ibid.

life, such as religious life or marriage, *is* a vocation; secondly, when we speak of a vocation *to* a state of life, such as religious life or marriage. The first extension of vocation is made insofar as the states of life are means that God gives us, by which he leads us to grow ever more in love for him, and finally to be perfectly united with him in glory. Thus they are paths through which he leads us to himself. In this way it is integral to the Catholic teaching on marriage to regard it as a Christian vocation. Marriage is unquestionably a means to grow in virtue and in love of God and neighbor, both due to its natural character, and as a sacrament. St. Thomas would therefore without hesitation recognize marriage as a vocation in this sense; he simply does not use vocation to refer to a state of life itself, whether the religious state or the married state.

The second extension of the term vocation is made insofar as God, by means of grace, the infused virtues, and the gifts of the Holy Spirit, does not lead and guide us only to the act of love itself, but also to the means by which we act in accordance with love, and grow in love. Thus whenever we are moved to a determinate action or choice by means of these grace-given virtues and gifts of the Spirit, we can say that we are called to that action or choice (though the word "call" tends to be more often used in reference to a more permanent state of life). Therefore when the love of God moves someone to commit himself to a state of life, we can say that he is called to that state of life. On the other hand, when someone is moved by other motives to a state of life, we cannot so properly say that he is called to that state.[36]

Therefore, if one can be moved by the love of God and neighbor to marriage, and if marriage is a means to grow in love of God and neighbor, then men and women are called to marriage, and marriage is a vocation. But one can marry out of true Christian love, and marriage is a means to grow in that love, and therefore marriage is a vocation, and some men and women are called to marriage. In our own times, Karol Wojtyła argues in this way that

36 This seems to be the import of St. Ignatius' note on divine vocation. "If one has not made his election duly and ordinately and without disordered tendencies... It does not appear that this election is a divine vocation, as being an election out of order and awry... for every divine vocation is always pure and clear, without mixture of flesh, or of any other inordinate tendency." *Exercitia Spiritualia*, n. 172.

marriage is a vocation insofar as it is, as it ought to be, a commitment made out of love.

> A vocation always means some principal direction of love of a particular man or woman... The process of self-giving remains most intimately united with spousal love. A person then gives himself to the other person. Therefore, both virginity and marriage understood in a deep personalistic way, are vocations.[37]

A further distinction should be made in regard to vocation in this sense. One can be moved by the love of God and neighbor to marriage in two ways: first, love of God could demand that one marry, or marriage could be most in accordance with this love; secondly, love of God could in fact be the motivation for one's marriage, without marriage being the choice most in accordance with this love. In the second way, everyone who loves God, since he loves him above all things, also orders marriage to the love of God, unless his desire or choice of marriage is sinful and disordered. This necessarily follows from the Catholic teaching that marriage is good. And it is true even of those many people who, in the words of St. Ignatius, "choose first to marry, which is a means, and secondarily to serve God our Lord in the married life, which service of God is the end."[38] Even these people at least virtually order their choice to God, and could actually do so. Nonetheless, love of God is not the *determining* factor in their choice.

Now to choose marriage in this way is not evil, but it is not the best way of choosing marriage. And recognition of this fact lies behind some of the seemingly negative statements about marriage that we may find in the Fathers and Doctors of the Church, statements which might seem to show a lack of esteem for marriage as a holy means for growing in and practicing love of God and neighbor. Many of these negative statements actually originate in a honest recognition of the fact that most people who choose to marry do not do so because they consider it the best means of serving God, but for other motives, and again, that many married persons do not order their whole married life to the love and service

---

37 *Love and Responsibility*, 256; cf. Pope John Paul II, General Audience of August 18, 1982.
38 *Exercitia Spiritualia*, n. 169.

44

of God. We should then not take these statements as denigrating marriage itself, but as criticisms of the material and worldly manner in which many marriages are lived.[39]

Love of God can also move someone to marriage in a different way, if one sees marriage not only as compatible with and capable of being ordered to the love of God, but as required by or at least most in accordance with this love. It does not necessarily follow from the Catholic teaching that marriage is good, that love of God demands that one marry, or even that marriage is often most in accordance with this love. And on this point, it does seem that St. Thomas, as well as St. Alphonsus and many other Doctors of the Church, considers it rare that marriage is most in accordance with perfect love of God, at least for those people who are capable of chastely abstaining from marriage.[40] Speaking about the necessity of perpetual chastity for perfection, St. Thomas remarks that it is presumptuous to suppose that one does not personally need the better means for attaining perfection, namely perfect chastity.

> The second way to perfection, by which a man may be
> more free to devote himself to God, and to cling more

---

39 One sometimes encounters a certain polemic in recent authors, directed against nearly the entire tradition of the Church, and convicting it of entirely failing to recognize the holiness of the human body and of marriage. One might get the impression that from the earliest times of the Church (including even the inspired Apostle Paul) until Pope John Paul II, no one in the Church really understood marriage, or had any appreciation for it as a holy Christian way of life. But though it is true that the earlier doctors of the Church made certain excesses and sometimes lacked certain insights, this sweeping dismissal of the Christian tradition is quite unjustified.

40 St. Augustine, *De Bono Conjugali,* n. 10, PL 40, 381; St. Jerome, *Adversus Jovinianum*, Bk. I, n. 9, PL 23, 233; St. Gregory the Great, *Regulae Pastoralis Liber*, Part III, Ch. 27, PL 77, 103–4; St. John Chrysostom, *De Virginitate*, n. 19 & 25, PG 48, 547 & 550, and Homily 19 on 1 Corinthians, PG 61, 153–54; St. Alphonsus, "Counsels to a young woman in doubt as to what state to choose" (see below, p. 48). The Fathers and Doctors generally cite St. Paul's teaching in 1 Corinthians in support of their position: "To the unmarried and the widows I say that it is well for them to remain single as I do. But if they cannot exercise self-control, they should marry. For it is better to marry than to be aflame with passion" (1 Cor 7:8–9).

perfectly to him, is the observance of perpetual
chastity... The way of continence is most necessary for
attaining perfection... Abraham had so great spiritual
perfection in virtue that his spirit did not fall short of
perfect love for God on account either of temporal
possessions or of married life. But if another man who
does not have the same spiritual virtue strives to attain
perfection while retaining riches and entering into
marriage, his error in presuming to treat Our Lord's
words as of small account will soon be demonstrated.[41]

Does this position regarding marriage necessarily follow
from the way that St. Thomas considers the ways of life, viz.
according to their suitability as means of attaining the Christian
goal? No, for though in general life according to the counsels is
better than the married life, in particular cases or for particular
persons marriage may be better. "Though it may be said in general
that for an individual man it is better to practice continence than to
enter into marriage, nothing prevents marriage from being better
for a particular person."[42] There are a number of reasons that would
in particular cases make marriage the best means for someone to
live out his vocation to love. First of all, there is the possibility that
God will give him evident miraculous signs that lead him to
marriage, or in some other way make it evident that he should do
so. In such a case, when God's will is made directly evident, then
one can and should follow his will as manifested, even if one
would otherwise have made a different judgment about what was
best and what God's will was. (This case corresponds to St.
Ignatius' first time for choosing a state of life.)

Secondly, some persons, on account of a special
relationship to the common good, can accomplish the most good
for the Church by marrying, and so are called to marriage. St.
Thomas does not explicitly mention this case, but it is in
accordance with his principles. St. Francis de Sales observes:

God does not want each person to observe all the
counsels, but only those that are appropriate to the
diversity of persons, times, occasions, and abilities, as
charity requires.... Perhaps you are a prince, by whose

---

41 *On the Perfection of the Spiritual Life*, Ch. 9.
42 St. Thomas Aquinas, *Summa Contra Gentiles*, 136.

posterity the subjects of your crown should be preserved in peace, and assured against tyranny, sedition, and civil wars; the occasion, therefore, of so great a good, obliges you to beget legitimate successors in a holy marriage.[43]

Thirdly, some persons are unable to live according to the counsels, either being incapable of really putting their heart into such a life, or for some other reason incapable of living such a life well. They will do better to live a life that they are capable of living, and of putting their heart into living as a way of serving God and neighbor, than to attempt to live a life of which they are not capable, or to which they are not able to give their whole heart.

> The evangelical counsels considered in themselves are advantageous for all; but due to some people being poorly disposed, it happens that they are not advantageous for these people, because their heart is not inclined to them. Hence the Lord, in proposing the evangelical counsels, always makes mention of man's fitness for observing the counsels. For in giving the counsel of perpetual poverty (Mt. 19:21), he begins by saying: "If you would be perfect," and then adds: "Go, sell all that you have." Similarly, in giving the counsel of perpetual chastity, when he said: "There are eunuchs who have made themselves eunuchs for the kingdom of heaven" (Mt. 19:12), he immediately added: "He who is able to receive this, let him receive it." And similarly the Apostle, after giving the counsel of virginity, says: "I say this for your benefit, not to lay any restraint upon you" (1 Cor. 7:35).[44]

This third category of persons called to marriage comprises by far the greatest number. There are some who see the beauty of the religious life, and consider living that life themselves, and may even enter for a time, yet who find themselves incapable of putting their heart wholly into such a life—in some cases they may see reasons why they are incapable of doing so, in other cases they may not see the reasons, but simply the fact. There are others who cannot even see the beauty and goodness of religious life in such a way as to be moved to love it; they may acknowledge its goodness

---

43 St. Francis de Sales, *Treatise on the Love of God*, Bk. 8, Ch. 6.
44 ST I-II 108:4 ad 1.

in an abstract manner, but not perceive it concretely, in such a way
that it draws their heart. While various natural and psychological
factors may contribute to this difference between persons, the
ultimate cause of the perception of religious life's beauty and
value, and the desire to live it, is from God. Pope John Paul II
interprets Christ's statement, "Not all men [can] grasp[45] this saying,
but only those to whom it is given," (Mat 19:11) in reference to this
necessary divine enlightenment.

> Jesus calls attention to the gift of divine light necessary
> to "understand" the way of voluntary celibacy. Not all
> can understand it, in the sense that not all are "able" to
> grasp its meaning, to accept it, to put it into practice.
> This gift of light and decision is only granted to some. It
> is a privilege granted them for the sake of a greater love.
> We should not be surprised then if many, not
> understanding the value of consecrated celibacy, are not
> attracted to it, and often are not even able to appreciate
> it. This means that there is a diversity of ways, charisms,
> and functions, as Saint Paul recognized, who
> spontaneously wished to share his ideal of virginal life
> with all. Indeed he wrote: "I wish that all were as I
> myself am. But each," he adds, "has his own gift from
> God, one of one kind and one of another" (1 Cor 7:7).[46]

There are several mistakes into which we can easily fall
when considering this question. One mistake is to think that every
person is called to the life according to the counsels, and that if he
chooses not to live this way, it is always due either to a lack of love
or virtue on his part, to presumption, or to ignorance. In other
words, either he does not love God enough to follow the better
path, he thinks he is already virtuous enough not to need the help of
the evangelical counsels, or he is ignorant that the counsels offer a
superior way to grow in the love of God. We might be led to this
position by an overly simple understanding of the necessity of the

45 The Revised Standard Version translates the text as, "can receive this."
The word used in Greek is χωροῦσιν, in Latin *capiunt,* in Italian
comprendere. All of these words can have the sense either of containing
or having capacity for something, or of understanding it. We have
translated it as "can grasp" in order to show this twofold possible
meaning.
46 Pope John Paul II, General Audience, November 16, 1994.

48

counsels, which are proposed universally as the better means for attaining Christian perfection and serving God. Thus St. Alphonsus says to a woman seeking advice, "If you resolve not to become a religious, I cannot advise you to enter the married state, for St. Paul does not counsel that state to any one, except in case of necessity, which I hope does not exist for you."[47] He seems to take the position that it is only better to marry if one is in fact incapable of being chaste without marriage. St. Thomas as well, perhaps as a result of reacting to those who deny the value of the counsels, may overstate the necessity of the counsels as a means for perfection, when he calls it presumptuous to seek perfection without embracing celibacy. (See above, page 44.)

A second mistake is to think that every person who marries has a vocation to marriage, or that it was the most perfect thing for him to do. In fact, many people choose to marry either without thinking about whether it is the best thing to do, or without caring. "Many choose first to marry, which is a means, and secondarily to serve God our Lord in the married life, which service of God is the end."[48] The renunciation asked by the evangelical counsels is difficult, and because many people are not willing to do all that is necessary in order to follow this path, or are in some other way led astray; "many are called, but few are chosen" (Mt. 22:14).

A third mistake is to make a comparison of marriage and religious life simply on the basis of the existence of diverse vocations—to consider the fact that marriage is better for some people, and they are called to marriage, and that religious life is better for others, and they are called to it—and thereby to conclude that the two ways are basically equally good ways of growing in virtue and in love. It is true that all are called to holiness, and that those who are called to marriage (in the stricter sense of vocation) will do better to marry than to enter religious life. But still, religious life offers to those who are called to it, a better means for attaining holiness. The Second Vatican Council, while remarking that seminarians "ought rightly to acknowledge the duties and dignity of Christian matrimony, which is a sign of the love between Christ and the Church," goes on to say that they should "recognize

---

47 St. Alphonsus, "Counsels to a young woman in doubt as to what state to choose" pp. 391–92.
48 *Exercitia Spiritualia*, n. 169.

the surpassing excellence of virginity consecrated to Christ."[49] Pope Paul VI, too, while noting the importance of promoting the universal call to holiness, warns against losing sight of the superiority of religious life.

> It must be admitted that the doctrine of the universal vocation of all the faithful to holiness (regardless of their position or social situation), has been put forth very much in modern times, and indeed rightly so... All these things are happening by the counsel of Divine Providence, and that is why We rejoice over such salutary undertakings.
>
> However, we must be on guard lest, for this very reason, the genuine notion of religious life as it has traditionally flourished in the Church, should become obscured, and youth, when they think about choosing of a way of life, be in some way hindered, due to their not distinctly and clearly perceiving the special function and immutable importance of the religious state within the Church... This state, which receives its proper character from profession of the evangelical vows, is a perfect way of living according to the example and teaching of Jesus Christ. It aims at the growth of charity, and its final perfection. In contrast, the specific ends, advantages and functions proposed in other ways of life, though they are legitimate in themselves, are temporal.[50]

The Church has always taught that the life according to the evangelical counsels is not only superior in itself, inasmuch as it is a life more like that of Christ himself, but also inasmuch as it is a better way to achieve the goal of Christian life, which is holiness. In *Vita Consecrata*, Pope John Paul II summarizes this tradition of the Church.

> The Church has always seen in the profession of the evangelical counsels a special path to holiness. The very expressions with which it describes it—the school of the Lord's service, the school of love and holiness, the way or state of perfection—indicate the effectiveness and the wealth of means which are proper to this form of

---

49 Vatican Council II, *Optatam Totius*, n. 10.
50 Pope Paul VI, Address to the General Chapters of Religious Orders and Congregations, May 23, 1964.

evangelical life, and the particular commitment made by those who embrace it. It is not by chance that there have been so many consecrated persons down the centuries who have left behind eloquent testimonies of holiness and have undertaken particularly generous and demanding works of evangelization and service.[51]

This teaching of the Church, that the counsels are better means for growing in love, is not merely an abstract and speculative truth. It is a practical truth that is very relevant to the question of whether to follow them or not. It is the reason why St. Ignatius says that more evident signs are required in order to conclude that God is calling one to ordinary Christian life in the world, than to conclude that God is calling one to embrace the evangelical counsels.[52] Again, one who does not know his vocation, but who could be called to religious life—i.e., could be called if if he is open to it, and disposes himself to receive the call—would do well to pray for this higher calling, and take other steps towards this goal. Again, some clearly see that marriage and religious life are both possible vocations for them, and in such cases the better choice is in general religious life. Von Balthasar gives a good description of some of these situations in which the one who is discerning may find himself.

> Many a youth, in considering his state, draws near the region of the special call; the call itself does not follow, but he knows that he is not forbidden from drawing ever closer to that region, in which the call may, or even probably will be heard. But he turns aside too soon, and consequently does not hear it... But it can also happen, that he moves into the region of the qualitatively superior call, draws within "calling range" of God, yet the call—by reason of its objective form, and not merely by reason of the imperfect way in which it is heard— allows him the choice to follow it or not to follow it. He sees quite factually: there is the usual way, and I am not forbidden to go along it. Yet this form of call lacks the magnetic attraction with which other forms draw one irresistibly to themselves.[53]

---

51 Pope John Paul II, *Vita Consecrata*, n. 35.
52 Directoria Ignatiana Autographa, n. 9, p. 72; see above, page 32.
53 Von Balthasar, *Christlicher Stand*, 353.

Advantage of the personal approach

As was said above, the point of departure St. Ignatius takes for considering the choice of a state of life is that of one who wants "to seek and find the divine will as to the management of his life for the salvation of his soul."[54] The attention to the divine will is so important that the one giving the exercises should not try to influence the one making the exercises, even to make a choice that is most excellent in itself, but should "allow the Creator to act immediately with the creature, and the creature with its Creator and Lord."[55]

St. Ignatius' approach to the choice of a state of a life, which puts the question in terms of seeking God's personal will for us, has the evident and substantial advantage of focusing on God as one with whom we are united in charity, the most proper act of which is to seek that which is pleasing to God.[56] Charity is a love of friendship with God. Now what distinguishes the love of friendship from other forms of love, is that "in the love of friendship, the lover is in the beloved insofar as he considers what is good or bad for his friend as good or bad for himself, and considers his friend's will as his own will."[57] Thus charity does not primarily seek God insofar as he is attainable by and good for us, but seeks God's own good in himself, and therefore also God's will, since the proper object of his will is his goodness. In his commentary on John's Gospel, St. Thomas explains the connection between love and obedience to God's will.

> Since to love someone is to will him good and to desire what he wills, he does not seem truly to love, who does not do the will of his beloved, and does not perform the things he knows that he wills. Therefore he who does not do the will of God, does not seem truly to love him; and therefore Christ says, "He who has my commandments and keeps them, is he who loves me" (Joh 14:21), that is, is he who has true love for me.[58]

---

54 *Exercitia Spiritualia*, n. 1.
55 *Exercitia Spiritualia*, n. 15.
56 Cf. *In III Sent*. d. 29, Explanation of Lombard's Text.
57 ST I-II 28:2.
58 St. Thomas Aquinas, *Super Evangelium Johannis*, Ch. 14, Lec. 5.

52

This attitude, of seeking God's will in all things, is better than the simple desire of attaining our own perfection and happiness. While it is true that God desires our sanctification and our perfection, and therefore to seek perfection is to seek what God seeks, this is not the best way to consider the matter, since love for our own perfection as such is love for ourselves, while love for our perfection as willed by God, is love for God. St. Francis de Sales remarks:

> The counsels are indeed given for the benefit of him who is counseled, so that he may be perfect: "If you would be perfect," said the Saviour, "go sell all that you have, and give it to the poor, and follow me." But the loving heart does not receive a counsel for its utility, but to conform itself to the desire of him who gives the counsel, and to render him the homage due to his will.[59]

To the extent that we possess more perfectly this attitude of charity, which seeks God's will more than its own, we can say with the Apostle St. Paul, "It is no longer I who live, but Christ who lives in me" (Gal 2:20). And St. Paul was even willing for a time (and perhaps altogether) to be separate from Christ, if that were to be pleasing to Christ's will. "I could wish that I myself were accursed and cut off from Christ for the sake of my brethren, my kinsmen by race" (Rom 9:3). St. John Chrysostom comments on this text of St. Paul:

> He means: on this account I am weary, and if I were to be separated from the company about Christ, and to be alienated, not from the love of him—that be far from him, since even all of this he was doing out of love—but from all that enjoyment and glory, I would accept it, provided my Master were not to be blasphemed... I would gladly lose even the kingdom and that unutterable glory, and undergo all necessary sufferings, as considering it the greatest consolation of all, no longer to hear him whom I so long for, so blasphemed.
>
> ... "For I could wish that I myself were accursed." What does the "I myself" mean? It means I who have been a teacher of all, who have gathered together countless good deeds, who am waiting for

---

59 St. Francis de Sales, *Treatise on the Love of God*, Bk. 8, Ch. 6.

countless crowns, who desired him so much, as to value his love above all things, who all my days am burning for him, and hold all things of second importance to the love of him. For even being loved by Christ was not the only thing he cared for, but loving him exceedingly also. And this last he cared most for.[60]

Potential disadvantage of the personal approach—apparently irreparable consequences of missteps in a vocation

If we consider the choice of a state of life as obedience to the will of God who calls us to that state, it seems that not choosing that state of life is direct disobedience to the will of God, and therefore a grave fault. And indeed, St. Ignatius suggests this in his directory dictated to P. Vitoria, where he indicates that sometimes a calling is so evident that one is under obligation to follow it.

> Not everyone can be a religious. The Lord says, "He who can take it, let him take it" (Mt 19:12), giving to be understood that there are some who cannot, and that those who can take it, if they want to be perfect, or in a certain sense even if they want simply to be saved, are obliged to take it, for it appears to be a precept inasmuch as he says, "He who can take it, let him take it"—in a case where they judge that they would be unable to keep the law of God our Lord in the world, or where the obviousness of their calling obliges them to follow it.[61]

Moreover, if we look at some of those who follow St. Ignatius' approach to vocation and the choice of a state of life, we can see a certain tendency to regard a vocation as involving a grave necessity of following it, and the failure to follow a vocation as a nearly irreparable mistake. We will consider in particular the positions of St. Alphonsus de Liguori, and Hans Urs von Balthasar.

---

60 Chrysostom, Homily 16 on the Epistle to the Romans, PG 60, 551–52.
61 Directorium Patri Vitoria Dicatum, n. 21, *Directoria*, p. 101.

St. Alphonsus

St. Alphonsus de Liguori asserts very emphatically the importance of following one's vocation; if one does not follow his vocation, it will be possible to live well, but extremely difficult.

> To enter into any state of life the divine vocation is necessary. For without this, if it is not impossible, it is at least most difficult to satisfy the obligations of that state and to be saved.[62]

St. Alphonsus gives two reasons for this. First, God in his providence has provided a certain path by which he desires one to attain salvation, and in which he has provided the means for attaining it. Thus, one who does not follow his vocation is not on the path intended by God, and does not have the means he ought to have for attaining salvation.

> It is clear that our eternal salvation depends principally on the choice of our state... In regard to choosing a state, if we want to make sure of our eternal salvation, we must follow the divine vocation, where alone God has prepared efficacious helps to save us... This is exactly the order of predestination described by the same Apostle: "He whom he predestined, he also called; and those whom he called, he also justified... and those he also glorified."... Upon vocation follows justification, and upon justification follows glorification, namely eternal life. He who places himself outside of this chain of salvation will not be saved. With all the efforts and with everything else that one will do, St. Augustine will say to him: "You run well, but outside of the way," namely outside of the way through which God will have called you to walk, in order to attain to your salvation. The Lord does not accept the sacrifices offered from one's own inclination: "For Cain and his offering he had no regard." Rather, he enjoins great punishment on those who want to turn their backs to their calls, to follow the plans of their own inclination: "Woe to the rebellious children," says the Lord through Isaiah, "who carry out a

---

62 St. Alphonsus, *Selva de materie predicabili*, Ch. 10, *Opere di S. Alfonso Maria de Liguori*, Vol. 3 (Torino: Marietti, 1880), 78.

plan, but not from me; and who make a league, but not by my spirit!"[63]

Secondly, one who does not follow his vocation despises God who calls him, and so is in turn punished by God with the loss of his light and grace for living well.

> Divine calls to a more perfect life are certainly special and very great graces that God does not give to all. Therefore he has much reason to be indignant with him who slights them. How offended does a prince consider himself, if he calls one of his vassals to serve him more closely and as his favorite in his palace, and he does not obey! And will not God resent it? Ah, only too much does he resent it and utter threats, saying, "Woe to him who strives with his maker!" "Woe" in the Scriptures signifies eternal perdition....
>
> To such as these, as rebels against the divine light (as the Holy Spirit says: "They were rebels against the light; they did not know his ways"), justly has been given the punishment of losing the light; and since they did not want to walk on the way indicated to them by the Lord, they will walk on the way chosen by their own will, without light, and thus they will perish... Therefore, when God calls to a more perfect state, he who does not want to put his eternal salvation in great danger, ought to obey, and obey quickly.[64]

Nevertheless, St. Alphonsus recognizes that sometimes God in his providence allows someone to choose a way of life without a vocation, for the sake of that person's own good. At least, he speaks of this possibility as regards a way of life that in itself is better, such as the religious or monastic life.

> You will answer me: "How can I be content, if I was not called to this state?" But what does it matter if at the beginning you were not called? Although you did not become a nun by divine vocation, it is nevertheless certain that God permitted that for your welfare; and if

63 St. Alphonsus, "Counsels Concerning a Religious Vocation," Ch. 1, pp. 396–97; see *Theologia Moralis*, Vol. 2, Bk. IV, Ch. 1, n. 78, edited by P. Leonardi Gaudé (Rome: Typographia Vaticana, 1907), 506–8.
64 St. Alphonsus, "Counsels Concerning a Religious Vocation," Ch. 1, pp. 397–98.

56

he did not call you then, at the present time he certainly
calls you to belong completely to him.[65]

St. Alphonsus is not very demanding in regard to the signs
of a vocation to religious life, however. As noted above, he
considers a good intention, the lack of obstacles, and acceptance by
superiors as sufficient signs of vocation.[66]

Von Balthasar

Von Balthasar similarly stresses the necessity of following
one's call, even though that to which one is called is not an
"obligation." The call is an expression of God's personal choice,
proceeding from his infinite love, and so to reject the call is to fail
in love. Indeed, it seems at times that the less obligation God
imposes of following his will, the more necessary it is to follow it.

> The more love reveals itself in the call, the less therefore
> this call can arm itself with its own sanctions, the more it
> is the expression of the defenseless, indeed the help-
> seeking love of God, which can offer no other argument
> for following it than the hope that the needs of love will
> be understood, then the more compelling it is—if he who
> is addressed is a lover—for him to give the needed
> answer.[67]

Von Balthasar recognizes at least the possibility that a call
from God may give a person complete freedom to follow it or not.
But at least in most cases, he considers it a pressing necessity of
love to follow God's call, and a grave failure in love, not to follow
it.

> There are perhaps calls that are scarcely anything more
> than a permission to go one way or the other. Such calls
> —supposing that there are such—may be ignored
> without fault... But as soon as one leaves behind these
> lowest ranking forms of vocation, and considers the
> cases that indeed according to the tradition are the most
> numerous, those in which God declares his personal
> choice to the soul, then other laws come into play, the

65 *The True Spouse of Jesus Christ*, Ch. 24, n. 8.
66 See page 33.
67 Von Balthasar, *Christlicher Stand*, 352.

laws of love. One must be very careful here with the maxim that only "precepts" bind under pain of sin, that one can heedlessly set aside wishes, invitations, whisperings of God's love. Does not God want to offer his best, perhaps his most important gifts more by asking than by demanding? And would not rejecting them mean injuring, perhaps rendering impossible the decisive plans of God's love?[68]

A vocation is a personal call from God, and therefore unique. One who does not follow his vocation cannot have another of his own choosing, but remains without a vocation in the proper sense.

We already said earlier that when one rejects the mission God had in mind for him, God does not give him another in its place. For missions are personal, and God does not speak the word that he saved for one man, indiscriminately to another....

Since the moment of the identity between the divine and the human "yes" should be the center that gives meaning to the life of the one called, this life, because that moment does not occur, necessarily remains unfulfilled, empty, a longing that has nothing more to wait for, like the life of an abandoned young woman, whose whole future has already passed her by.[69]

The harm done is nearly irreparable. Even if one repents, and confesses his failure, the loss and the damage done by the rejection of the call remains.

The fundamental "No" with which they once responded to their mission, even if confessed as a sin and forgiven, remains as an emptiness in their soul, and leads them to many a fault that otherwise would have remained undone.[70]

The consequences are most serious even in the case of one who almost unconsciously, and with little fault on his part turned away from his call.

---

68 Ibid., 407.
69 Ibid., 408 & 410.
70 Ibid., 412.

58

When the rejection lay on the border of the unconscious and therefore of blamelessness, then it can become the life of a man, which for him himself remains inexplicably unfulfilled. He is haunted by misfortune. He would, perhaps, like to marry, but the engagement miscarries; the girl refuses, without his understanding why. He tries again later, it again fails. His undertakings do not blossom. Either he gets no children, or death takes them from him. He doesn't succeed as others do, to gain a foothold and to establish himself in life without worries. A disquiet fills him, more laid upon him by fortune than deriving from his character. Among the men of the world he remains a stranger and feels like one. People will not explain to him the true reason for his unsettled state, so as not to deprive him of hope. Perhaps God will have pity on him, and grant him peace.[71]

Von Balthasar here is speaking primarily of what he calls the "qualitatively superior" call, the call to the life of the evangelical counsels. However, the reasons he gives for the importance of following the call are: (1) the personal character of the call; (2) the inner need of love to respond to love. Therefore, if the call to the lay state, the call to marriage, is a personal call (even if on his account, it must be described as a "not-being-called" in a higher way), and asks for a response of love, then the same consequences will follow for one who does not follow a vocation to marriage or some other lay vocation; his life also will remain empty and unfulfilled.

Explanation of this grave necessity

In both St. Alphonsus and von Balthasar, the urgent necessity of following a vocation and the dire consequences of failing to do so, are based upon what we might call the "personalistic" approach to vocation. The idea in each case seems to be that God has one personal plan for each individual, in which alone he would find his fulfillment, salvation, and happiness. St. Alphonsus states: "If we want to make sure of our eternal salvation, we must follow the divine vocation, where alone God prepares for

---

71 Ibid., 410.

us the efficacious means for us to save ourselves."[72] Von Balthasar likewise says:

> Would not rejecting them mean injuring, perhaps rendering impossible the decisive plans of God's love? ... When one rejects the mission that God had in mind for him, God does not give him another in its place. For missions are personal, and God does not speak the word that he saved for this man, indiscriminately to another man.[73]

Consequently, one who fails to follow a vocation is practically speaking unable to be fulfilled and happy. And according to St. Alphonsus, it seems, he will find it difficult even to be saved.

> The punishment of the disobedient will begin already during his lifetime, when he will always be restless; for Job says, "Who has resisted him and had peace?" Hence he will be deprived of the abundant and efficacious helps for living well. Therefore the Theologian Habert wrote: "Not without great difficulties will he be able to look out for his salvation." With great difficulty will he be saved, being forever like a member out of its proper place, so that only with great difficulty will he be able to live well... Therefore he concludes that "although absolutely speaking he could be saved, he will with difficulty enter the way, and lay hold of the means of salvation."... Therefore, when God calls to a more perfect state, he who does not want to put his eternal salvation in great danger ought to obey, and obey quickly.[74]

Though von Balthasar insists that we can never despair of the salvation of such persons,[75] he has similar dire things to say about the consequences of rejecting a divine calling.

> A hundred times would they have thrown the silver pieces into the temple, but their repentance does not

---

72 St. Alphonsus, "Counsels Concerning a Religious Vocation," Ch. 1, p. 396.

73 Von Balthasar, *Christlicher Stand*, 407–8.

74 St. Alphonsus, "Counsels Concerning a Religious Vocation," Ch. 1, pp. 397–98.

75 See von Balthasar, *Christlicher Stand*, 354–55 & 410–11.

make what happened not have happened. They are "cut off" as an example for all the others, that these may not become proud, but stand in awe (Rom 11:19–20). That they are cut off and burn, does not mean that they are going to be ultimately lost, just that they have played out their role on earth...

They who perhaps thought, in place of the divine mission, to exercise a meaningful role in the world and a corresponding influence as a lay apostle, see gradually how their life dries up and—what for them is the worst, and the punishment—sinks into meaninglessness... Had God destined them for the lay state, they would have borne, in the place meant for them, the hidden but living fruit that God expected of them. But as it is, their life is wasted, and they consume themselves in unfruitful criticism, especially of the Church, without contributing to its betterment.[76]

The second reason for this strong position seems to be that God speaks his plan personally to the one called, as a kind of love proposal—and so to reject this plan is to turn away from God's most intimate offer of love. St. Alphonsus says: "Divine calls to a more perfect life are certainly special and very great graces that God does not give to all. Therefore he has much reason to be indignant with him who slights them."[77] And von Balthasar, in some measure criticizing the traditional concept or understanding of "counsels," says that the less obligatory God's proposal is, the more urgent is the need to follow it.

The word "counsel" is not wholly adequate to convey God's personal love that lies in the invitation to personal discipleship.... God's predilection, by which he calls a man, and offers him the grace of receiving insight into and participation in the deeper mysteries of the divine love, is affected in a different way by the discourtesy of a rejection than if one transgressed what one considered a formal "law." But that means at the same time, that the transformation of the call from a predominantly commanding tone to a predominantly inviting tone, may

---

76 Von Balthasar, *Christlicher Stand*, 410–412.
77 St. Alphonsus, "Counsels Concerning a Religious Vocation," Ch. 1, p. 397.

in no way be interpreted as a weakening of its urgency. On the contrary, the more love reveals itself in the call, the less therefore this call can arm itself with its own sanctions.... then when he who is addressed is a lover, the more urgent for him is the needed answer.[78]

It does not necessarily follow that when God's loving proposal is rejected, God will not continue for long to pursue such an intimate love. However, normally this seems to be the natural conclusion of this way of thinking. St. Alphonsus states that one should obey a call quickly, since God's enlightenment will not remain.

> When God calls to a more perfect state, he who does not want to put his eternal salvation in great danger ought to obey, and obey quickly. Otherwise he will hear himself reproached by Jesus Christ as he reproached that youth, who, invited to follow him, said: "I will follow you Lord, but let me first take leave of those who are at home." And Jesus answered him, that he was not fit for paradise: "No one putting his hand to the plow, and looking back, is fit for the kingdom of God." The lights of God are passing, not permanent. Hence St. Thomas Aquinas says that vocations to a more perfect life should be followed as quickly as possible.[79]

Von Balthasar says that generally God does not indefinitely pursue one who neglects his call, and that he does not give a second call to one who refuses the first.

> Neither here nor in the vocation itself are there universally valid norms: every way is a new, unrepeatable love story... And yet the case of the rich young man is surely the more frequent case: God makes

---

78 Von Balthasar, *Christlicher Stand*, 352.

79 St. Alphonsus, "Counsels Concerning a Religious Vocation," Ch. 1, p. 398. St. Alphonsus may actually be quoting St. Thomas out of context. In ST II-II 189:3, St. Thomas says that a person "is bound to enter as soon as possible." However, he is there speaking about someone who made a vow to enter religious life. In general, St. Thomas does not think it necessary to delay entering a religious community, if one has no impediments, but he does not say that one is obliged to enter immediately, nor does he exclude the possibility of there sometimes being good reasons for delaying.

his invitation once, perhaps several times, but finally lets go of the soul that repudiates God's friendship. With that, the episode of God's courtship with this life is essentially at an end; not that we should despair of the salvation of this man, since he is constantly offered sufficient grace to save himself, but indeed, the chance to become a chosen friend of God is spoiled forever. God does not twice give a special, privileged mission; he can certainly wait until the man finally makes up his mind for the decisive choice, but if the choice is negative, then repentance will no longer help.[80]

This position taken by St. Alphonsus and von Balthasar, as well as by others who adopt the same approach, is a somewhat natural conclusion of their way of approaching the question of vocation. However, it is not a necessary conclusion, and in fact is based on an implicitly anthropomorphic view of God's dealings with us. As regards the first point, God's personal plan for each of us, it is true that God knows and loves each man in all his personality and particularity. God deals personally with each man, and each man has his specific place in divine providence—"all things work for good for those who love God" (Rom 8:28)—yet at the same time, God is infinite and eternal, and sees all things simultaneously. So also his providence includes all things, even our sins and mistakes. God does not make plans merely on the basis of present conditions, as we do, so that his plans could be frustrated by men's consequent refusal to follow God's commands or invitations. All of men's choices were included in his plan from eternity. For example, if a man is called to religious life, but like the rich young man in the gospel, he is unwilling to give something up, and he falls in love with a woman and marries her, his choice and his marriage were in God's providential plan from the beginning. And God for his part will provide the graces the man needs to live marriage well. If the marriage is especially difficult, it will be because of circumstances or because he was not suited for that marriage, not because God spitefully denies him the grace he needs in the married state, because he wanted him to choose another state of life. To take another example, if a Christian woman marries a non-Christian man unwisely and without being called to

---

80 Von Balthasar, *Christlicher Stand*, 354–55.

such a marriage, and has great difficulty in living a Christian life in this marriage, she does not have difficulty because God denies her grace due to her having chosen the marriage without a vocation to it, but due to the character of the persons and the marriage itself.

As regards the second point, that God's love proposal is not continued indefinitely, it is true that as regards specific callings, God does not normally continue to call someone indefinitely. Usually he stops when the person becomes deaf to the call, or an obstacle intervenes—for example, when someone called to celibacy marries, God no longer calls him to celibacy. But as regards his calling men to union with himself, God never ceases to call anyone as long as they are in this life. For God "desires all men to be saved and to come to the knowledge of the truth" (1 Tim 2:4), and wills their sanctification (cf. 1 Th 4:3). "All the faithful, whatever their condition or state, are called by the Lord, each in his own way, to that perfect holiness whereby the Father Himself is perfect."[81] *All* the faithful, whether they entered into their state through a divine vocation, or by neglecting their vocation, are called not only to salvation, but to perfect holiness.

All this is not to say that the choice of a state of life is not a very serious matter, and of decisive importance. It is only to say that the reason for its particular importance lies not so much on God's part, as on the part of the state itself—the fact that it is permanent, and that it affects all aspects of one's life. Though one cannot thwart God's plan, and one is never abandoned by God, and is always given grace to attain holiness, the state of life itself remains. Hence, if one is poorly suited to that state, one will have more difficulty in fulfilling its duties and in making spiritual progress than if one were in a state to which one was well suited.

Moreover, to the degree that one perceives more surely and concretely the good to be accomplished in embracing a state of life, the more responsible one may be for failing to do so. Thus Pope John Paul II, though he points out that Christ did not condemn the rich young man who refused Christ's call to follow him,[82] notes the serious consequences that the failure to follow a call may entail.

---

81 Vatican Council II, *Lumen Gentium*, Ch. 2, n. 11.
82 General Audience, October 12, 1994.

64

> This, in fact, is a vocation: a proposal, an invitation, or
> rather a concern to bring the Savior to the world of
> today, which needs him so much. A refusal would mean
> not only rejecting the Lord's word, but also abandoning
> many of our brothers and sisters in horror, in
> meaninglessness, or in the frustration of their most secret
> and noble aspirations, to which they neither know how
> to nor are able to respond alone.[83]

The saying of St. Ignatius, that there are cases in which the vocation is so manifest that one is "under obligation to follow it,"[84] might be interpreted on the basis of this principle. In other words, if the possibility of doing great spiritual good for others is experienced not merely as a possibility, but as a concrete and definite proposal made immediately by God, then one may well be obliged to seek to do this good—as in general one is obliged to help a fellowman in immediate danger of his life or of grave spiritual harm.

83 Pope John Paul II, Homily, December 20, 1981; cf. *Pastores Dabo Vobis*, n. 36.
84 Directorium Patri Vitoria Dicatum, n. 21, *Directoria*, p. 101. See above, page 53.

Chapter 4: The Popes on Vocation

Pope John Paul II

Pope John Paul II takes primarily the "personalistic" approach to vocation, yet combines it in some measure with the "objective" approach, thus avoiding some of the problems that can arise for the personal approach. It will therefore be helpful for us to examine his view of vocation. First of all, a vocation is the means by which God directs every single person to his task in life. "Jesus has a specific task in life for each and every one of us. Each one of us is hand-picked, called by name by Jesus! There is no one among us who does not have a divine vocation!"[1] While some are called audibly by God, the calling is usually internal. "What is a vocation? It is an interior call of grace, which falls into the soul like a seed, to mature within it."[2]

It is not possible to give a universal account of how a vocation is experienced, since "apart from the universal elements that are found in every vocation, each call takes place concretely in ways that are always new and always different—and let us add, always beautiful and wonderful, because God is always wonderful in all that he does."[3] However, a general outline can be drawn, and the Pope does so in several places—usually in regard to religious vocation, but sometimes in regard to the vocation of any Christian.

> Do not be slow to answer the Lord's call! From the passage of the Book of Exodus read to us in this Mass we can learn how the Lord acts in every vocation (cf. Ex 3:1–6, 9–12). First, he provokes a new awareness of his presence—the burning bush. When we begin to show an interest he calls us by name. When our answer becomes

---

1   Pope John Paul II, Homily of June 1, 1982; cf. *Redemptor Hominis*, n. 21.
2   Pope John Paul II, Angelus, December 14, 1980.
3   Pope John Paul II, Homily of September 7, 1986; cf. *Redemptor Hominis*, n. 21.

more specific and like Moses we say: "Here I am" (cf. v. 4), then he reveals more clearly both himself and his compassionate love for his people in need. Gradually he leads us to discover the practical way in which we should serve him: "I will send you." And usually it is then that fears and doubts come to disturb us and make it more difficult to decide. It is then that we need to hear the Lord's assurance: "I am with you" (Ex 3:12). Every vocation is a deep personal experience of the truth of these words: "I am with you."[4]

The Pope often describes the process by which someone is called as a dialogue between the person and Christ.

In the hidden recesses of the human heart the grace of a vocation takes the form of a dialogue. It is a dialogue between Christ and an individual, in which a personal invitation is given. Christ calls the person by name and says: "Come, follow me." This call, this mysterious inner voice of Christ, is heard most clearly in silence and prayer. Its acceptance is an act of faith.[5]

This is a description of the grace of a religious vocation—a vocation to the religious life or priesthood. The description can, however, be basically applied to other vocations, though in other vocations the force of the "personal invitation" may be less. The vocation to marriage is not so much experienced as an invitation by Christ to give one's love and oneself to another human being; nevertheless, the decision to marry should be made with full consciousness of the meaning and purpose of marriage in relation to Christ and his church. Consequently, marriage is also a vocation that should be discerned in prayer.[6]

The Pope also often explains vocations by means of an analogy with the vocation of the prophet Jeremiah, which the Pope calls a "universal model" for every vocation.[7] God's word comes to Jeremiah and announces to him: "Before I formed you in the womb

---

4 Pope John Paul II, Homily, January 13, 1995.
5 Pope John Paul II, Homily February 10, 1986; cf. *Pastores Dabo Vobis*, n. 36.
6 See Homily of December 15, 1994.
7 Pope John Paul II, Homily of September 7, 1986; cf. *Pastores Dabo Vobis*, n. 36, and *Vita Consecrata*, n. 19.

I knew you, and before you were born I consecrated you; I appointed you a prophet to the nations" (Jer 1:5). Thus begins a dialogue between God and Jeremiah. The Pope uses this description of Jeremiah's calling to illustrate the way God calls each person.

> The Lord tells the Prophet Jeremiah that his vocation was part of God's eternal plan even before he was born... These words remind us that each person has a place in God's plan and that each of us should carefully listen to God's voice in prayer in order to discover the special calling we have received in Christ.[8]

But is the decision of vocation to be made only on the basis of prayer? Does "listening to God's voice in prayer" mean an introverted examination of our experiences of prayer? No, for "in many other ways too we learn to know God's will: through important events in our lives, through the example and wisdom of others, and through the prayerful judgment of his Church."[9] All that one learns of oneself and of the world in which one lives, are at least potential factors informing this decision. In his letter to youth for the "International Year of Youth," the pope describes the process by which God's call becomes the plan or path for a person's life:

> We could speak here of the "life" vocation, which in a way is identical with that plan of life which each of you draws up in the period of your youth... This "plan" is a "vocation" inasmuch as in it there make themselves felt the various factors which call. These factors usually make up a particular order of values (also called a "hierarchy of values"), from which emerges an ideal to be realized, an ideal which is attractive to a young heart. In this process the "vocation" becomes a "plan," and the plan begins to be also a vocation.
>
> ...During youth a person puts the question, "What must I do?" not only to himself and to other people from whom he can expect an answer, especially his parents and teachers, but he puts it also to God, as his Creator and Father. He puts it in the context of this

---

8   Pope John Paul II, Homily of September 2, 1990.
9   Ibid.

particular interior sphere in which he has learned to be in a close relationship with God, above all in prayer. He therefore asks God: "What must I do?", what is your plan for my life? Your creative, fatherly plan? What is your will? I wish to do it.

In this context the "plan" takes on the meaning of a "life vocation," as something which is entrusted by God to an individual as a task. Young people, entering into themselves and at the same time entering into conversation with Christ in prayer, desire as it were to read the eternal thought which God the Creator and Father has in their regard. They then become convinced that the task assigned to them by God is left completely to their own freedom, and at the same time is determined by various circumstances of an interior and exterior nature. Examining these circumstances, the young person, boy or girl, constructs his or her plan of life and at the same time recognizes this plan as the vocation to which God is calling him or her.[10]

The pope here describes the part of the process that actually determines one's choice of vocation as one that relies upon "objective" circumstances, both interior and exterior. "[Their task] is determined by various circumstances of an interior and exterior nature." These circumstances vary from individual to individual, and therefore a complete description cannot be given. However, the primary interior circumstance can be summed up with a single word—love. "Love is the fundamental and innate vocation of every human being,"[11] and consequently, as was said above, having a vocation means being drawn by love and in love to commit oneself to a way of life. Thus the Pope reasons that marriage is a vocation by reason of the love to which it is called.

According to God's will, the family has been established as "an intimate partnership of life and love" (Vatican Council II, *Gaudium et spes*, n. 48). It has been sent to become more and more what it is, that is, a partnership of life and love. Thus, a person's life decision for marriage and the family is a response to a personal call

---

10 Pope John Paul II, *Dilecti Amici*, n. 9.
11 Pope John Paul II, *Familiaris Consortio*, n. 11.

from God. It is a genuine vocation, which includes a mission.[12]

In his work which he wrote before he became pope, *Love and Responsibility*, he defines a vocation precisely in terms of such a commitment in love.

> The word "vocation" indicates that there exists for every person a proper direction of his development through the commitment of his entire life in the service of certain values... And therefore a vocation always means some principal direction of love of a particular man.[13]

Since man's vocation "consists in the sincere gift of self,"[14] and it is through love that one gives himself, the love of a man and woman for each other, if it is a true love, can be the beginning of the vocation to marriage. In his letter to youth, the pope goes on to describe this important relationship between love and vocation:

> [The difference, equal dignity, and complementarity of masculinity and femininity] is a theme that is necessarily inscribed in the personal "I" of each one of you. Youth is the period when this great theme affects in an experiential and creative way the soul and body of every young woman and young man, and becomes manifest within the conscience, together with knowledge of the self in all its manifold potentiality. Then also on the horizon of a young heart a new experience occurs: the experience of love, which from the beginning asks to be included in that plan of life which youth spontaneously creates and forms.... Through *that love* which is born in you—and is included in the plan and aim of your whole life—you must see God, who is love (1 John 4:8).
>
> And so I ask you not to break off your conversation with Christ in this extremely important phase of your youth; I ask you rather to commit yourselves even more. When Christ says "Follow me," his call can mean: "I call you to still another love"; but very often it can mean: "Follow me," follow me who am the Bridegroom of the Church, who is my bride; come,

12 Pope John Paul II, Address to the members of the Schönstatt Family Association, April 17, 1998.
13 *Love and Responsibility*, 229.
14 Pope John Paul II, *Evangelium Vitae*, n. 25.

70

you too become the bridegroom of your bride, you too become the bride of your spouse. Both of you become sharers in that mystery, that Sacrament, which the Letter to the Ephesians says is something great: great "in reference to Christ and the Church" (Eph 5:32).[15]

Similarly, the vocation to the total gift of self in the religious life depends upon love. Considered in itself, the state of Christian virginity or celibacy is preferable to that of marriage, since this state "frees the heart of man in a unique fashion (cf. 1 Cor. 7:32–35) so that it may be more inflamed with love for God and for all men,"[16] However, in order to really accomplish this function and to serve this end, it must be embraced with the proper motivation, namely "for the sake of the kingdom of heaven," (Mt. 19:12) and be embraced wholeheartedly as a way of giving oneself entirely to God. For this reason, Pope John Paul II says that the choice of celibacy must be a well-considered and deeply motivated choice.

On man's part an act of deliberate will is required, aware of the duty and of the privilege of consecrated celibacy. It is not a question of simply abstaining from marriage, nor an unmotivated and almost passive observance of the norms imposed by chastity. The act of renunciation has a positive aspect in the total dedication to the kingdom, which implies absolute devotion to God "who is supremely loved" and to the service of his kingdom. Therefore, the choice must be well-thought out and stem from a firm, conscious decision that has matured deep within the individual.[17]

The evangelical counsel of chastity, the counsel that "most obviously shows the power of grace, which raises love beyond the human being's natural inclinations,"[18] requires a special gift of God in order to be embraced. It requires a special love to make this whole hearted dedication of oneself in virginity or celibacy as a means for growing in love of God and serving one's neighbor—and as was said above, this whole hearted dedication is the most

15 Pope John Paul II, *Dilecti Amici*, n. 10.
16 Vatican II, *Perfectae Caritatis*, n. 12.
17 Pope John Paul II, General Audience, November 16, 1994.
18 Ibid.

important thing in any way of life. To devote oneself wholeheartedly to a life of virginity or celibacy requires a special charism, a grace of enlightenment and movement of the heart which is not given to all, a special "mode" of divine love, which disposes one to devote oneself exclusively to Christ and his church, and enables one to make a firm choice of this way of life. This charism is not to be understood as an essentially higher degree of love, as though all who embrace the virginal or celibate state love God more than those who do not embrace this state. Nor is this charism to be understood by way of subtraction, as though those called to belong wholly to Christ were either incapable of making a gift of themselves to another human being in marriage, or were not inclined to do so. A lack of the natural inclination towards marriage could even impede the virginal or celibate self-giving to Christ and his church. This charism is rather to be understood by way of an addition to the love, which specifies the love, giving it a more completely spousal *mode*. Those who are called to this state experience or possess the love of Christ or their neighbor in such a way that they are enabled to make this wholehearted gift of themselves.[19] In his series of catecheses on the theology of the body, Pope John Paul II also points out how the dedication of one's body in consecrated virginity or celibacy is the expression of spousal love for Christ.

---

19 It is not possible to give a universal description of this love except in relation to its effect, viz. that it leads someone to give himself entirely to Christ. For some the path to such dedication begins simply with spousal love for Christ himself, really analogous to the spousal love of a man and a woman for each other in marriage. For others it begins with a particularly intense love of their fellow men, and a desire to bring God to them. For still others the love itself is perhaps not experienced in a special way, but they perceive more concretely how the counsel of continence can be a means to further this love of God, and this perception is enough for them to make a firm choice of celibacy. Historically, people would also sometimes choose religious life (which always includes celibacy) simply in order to be more sure of their own salvation. While this is not the best of motives, and the Church now seems to consider this motive in need of purification (See *Directives on Formation in Religious Institutes*, Congregation for Institutes of Consecrated Life and Societies of Apostolic Life, February 2, 1990, n. 89), it would be going too far to say that such people did not have a vocation to religious life, or that they were acting contrary to God's will.

It is a characteristic feature of the human heart to accept even difficult demands in the name of love, for an ideal, and above all *in the name of love for a person* (love is, in fact, oriented by its very nature toward the person). And so, in this call to continence "for the kingdom of heaven," first the disciples and then the whole living tradition of the Church quickly discovered the love *for Christ himself as the Bridegroom of the Church, Bridegroom of souls*, to whom he has given himself to the end (cf. Jn 13:1; 19:30) in the mystery of his Passover and of the Eucharist.

In this way, continence "for the kingdom of heaven," the choice of virginity or celibacy for one's whole life, has become in the experience of the disciples and followers of Christ the act of *a particular response to the love* of the Divine Bridegroom, and therefore *acquired the meaning of an act of spousal love*, that is, of a spousal gift of self with the purpose of answering in a particular way the Redeemer's spousal love; a gift of self understood as a *renunciation*, but realized above all *out of love.*[20]

At the root of this spousal love is a particular enlightenment of the mind and heart, an enlightenment that has its origin in God. This enlightenment, which is a way of God speaking to the heart, belongs in some manner to every vocation, and can even be called an interior vocation.

St. Augustine does not see in this resolution the fulfillment of a divine precept, but a vow freely taken. In this way it was possible to present Mary as an example to "holy virgins" throughout the Church's history....

The Angel does not ask Mary to remain a virgin, it is Mary who freely reveals her intention of virginity. In this commitment is found her choice of love that leads her to dedicate herself totally to the Lord by a life of virginity.

In stressing the spontaneity of Mary's decision, we should not forget that God's initiative is at the origin of every vocation. In directing herself to the life of virginity, the maiden of Nazareth was responding to an interior vocation, that is, to an inspiration of the Holy

---

20 Pope John Paul II, General Audience, April 21, 1982.

Spirit that enlightened her about the meaning and value
of the virginal gift of herself.[21]

Referring to this special gift, Christ says of the counsel of
continence, "Not all can accept it, but only those to whom it is
given," (Mt 19:10) and St. Paul says, "Each has his own special gift
from God, one of one kind and one of another" (1 Cor 7:7). As we
mentioned above (p. 47), a certain perception or understanding of
this way of life is necessary in order to desire it and to devote
oneself to it. In his catecheses, Pope John Paul II notes that the
necessary understanding is not a dry and abstract understanding,
but one that is living and concrete.

> Christ speaks about an understanding ("Not all can
> understand it, but only those to whom it has been
> granted," Mt 19:11); and it is not a question of an
> "understanding" in the abstract, but an understanding
> that influences the decision, the personal choice in which
> the "gift," that is, the grace, must find an adequate
> resonance in the human will.[22]

In summary, a vocation begins with Christ, who makes an
approach in love to an individual person, leading him to search for
a path in life by which to respond to Christ's love. In prayerful
dialogue with Christ, this person then examines his personal
circumstances, in order to find the path of life in which he can
make the best gift of himself in love.

This is, however, a kind of ideal situation, to which the
concrete decisions of persons do not always correspond. Many
choose a path in life without reference to Christ or to their
vocation. Does that mean, then, that they do not have any vocation?
No, for though they did not enter into their state in order to fulfill

---

21 Pope John Paul II, General Audience, August 7, 1996. The pope goes on
to say that "no one can accept this gift without feeling called." This
should not, however, be taken too literally. What the pope seems to have
in mind, is that such a gift of oneself to God is always a response to God,
who first loves a person, and desires in love to draw that person to
himself. Nevertheless it is not true as a matter of experience, that
everyone who embraces virginity out of love for God *feels* called.
22 Pope John Paul II, General Audience of March 31, 1982.

the will of God, God still has a mission which he wants them to fulfill in the state which they have chosen.[23]

Pope Benedict XVI

Pope Benedict XVI takes basically the same starting point as Pope John Paul II. God has a personal plan for each of us, and we must listen to him to learn what it is.

> The Lord has his plan for each of us, he calls each one of us by name. Our task is to be listeners, capable of perceiving his call, to be courageous and faithful, so that we may follow him, and in the end, be found as trustworthy servants who have used well the gifts entrusted to us.[24]

The origin and goal of this plan is God's love. God loves us, so that we can love him in return. "He loves us, he makes us see and experience his love, and from God's loving us 'first,' love can also arise as a response within us."[25] A vocation is always situated in the context of this love. "Before the creation of the world, before our coming into existence, the heavenly Father chose us personally, calling us to enter into a filial relationship with him, through Jesus, the Incarnate Word, under the guidance of the Holy Spirit."[26]

God's voice inviting us to love him is heard in the people and events around us, but especially in prayer. In response to a question by a seminarian about how one can discern God's voice calling one, the pope gives the following answer:

> God speaks with us in many different ways. He speaks by means of others, through friends, parents, pastors, priests.... He speaks by means of the events of our life, in which we can discern God's gesture; he speaks also through nature, creation, and he speaks, naturally and above all, in his Word, in Sacred Scripture, read in the

---

23 Pope John Paul II, Homily January 24, 1982.

24 Pope Benedict XVI, Homily for the Marian Vespers with the Religious and Seminarians of Bavaria, September 11, 2006.

25 Pope Benedict XVI, *Deus Caritas Est*, n. 17.

26 Pope Benedict XVI, Message for 43rd World Day of Prayer for Vocations, May 7, 2006.

communion of the Church and read personally in conversation with God. It is important to read Sacred Scripture, on the one hand in a very personal way... as God's Word which is ever timely and speaks to me... to enter into prayer and thus read Sacred Scripture as a conversation with God.[27]

Again, Pope Benedict XVI sees love as an important, indeed *the* element in a vocation. It is at the origin of every vocation, and every vocation finds its fulfillment in love. Thus the pope describes marriage as a vocation insofar as it is to be formed by true love.

If you are engaged to be married, God has a project of love for your future as a couple and as a family.... The love of a man and woman is at the origin of the human family and the couple formed by a man and a woman has its foundation in God's original plan (cf *Gen* 2:18–25).... In your prayer together, ask the Lord to watch over and increase your love and to purify it of all selfishness. Do not hesitate to respond generously to the Lord's call, for Christian matrimony is a true and proper vocation in the Church.[28]

The ways in which God's love arouses a response of love, the forms a vocation takes, can be very diverse: a vocation may be experienced as a manifest external call, or it may simply be experienced as an inner desire to give oneself to God. Distinguishing the apostles from Mary Magdalene and others, Pope Benedict XVI says that the latter followed Christ "on their own initiative."

In the course of the centuries so many men and women, transformed by divine love, have consecrated their own existence to the cause of the Kingdom. Already on the shores of the Sea of Galilee, many let themselves be won by Jesus: they were in search of healing in body or spirit, and they were touched by the power of his grace. Others were chosen personally by him and became his apostles. We also find some, like Mary Magdalene and other

---

27 Pope Benedict XVI, Address to the Seminarians of the Roman Major Seminary, February 17, 2007.
28 Pope Benedict XVI, Message for 22nd World Youth Day, 2007.

women, who followed him on their own initiative, simply out of love. But like the disciple John, they too filled a special place in his heart. These men and women, who through Jesus knew the mystery of the Father's love, represent the variety of vocations which have always been present in the Church.[29]

In speaking of those who follow Jesus "on their own initiative," he differs from Pope John Paul II, who is always careful to avoid such language. But in this, Pope Benedict seems to follow more closely the actual diverse experiences that people have of vocations.

---

29 Pope Benedict XVI, Message for 43rd World Day of Prayer for Vocations, May 7, 2006.

Chapter 5: Conclusions

Having considered the two contrasting approaches to vocation, represented by St. Thomas Aquinas and St. Ignatius of Loyola, and a somewhat intermediate view represented by Pope John Paul II, let us now draw from these considerations some principles that can be used to gain, as far as is possible, the advantages of each approach.

(1) First, the aim of all considerations and choices should be to do the will of God and to draw close to him. Therefore also the decision to enter a state of life should be made in light of this aim, and in the presence of Christ, in prayer. However, normally God's will is not immediately manifested to us, but it is the will of God, who created us as rational creatures, that we should decide our path using our mind and our heart.

(2) Thus, secondly, the ordinary means by which we should make a choice of a state of life is by a consideration of our situation, placed in the light of faith, and animated by love. "When a prudent man listens to his conscience," which is a judgment about what to do in a concrete situation, "he can hear God speaking."[1] So it is also in the choice of a state of life: the Christian usually finds God's will by means of loving and prudent reflection. (3) Among the circumstances involved in our situation, both subjective and objective factors are important, since the value of what we choose is important, and the attitude we have towards it is important. (4a) It is absolutely necessary that the state we choose be good and holy in itself, if our choice is to be good. (4b) But after this, the most important factor is the subjective attitude with which we are going to approach that state, i.e., how fully we will use that state as a means to the goal of doing God's will, drawing close to him ourselves, and bringing others to him. (5) Of the various particular elements that affect how capable we are of devoting ourselves to a way of life, love is the most significant.

---

1 *Catechism of the Catholic Church*, n. 1777.

In summary:

1. The beginning of our consideration, and the aim, should be God and his will.

2. The process for making a decision should be based on the facts about ourselves, God, and the needs and circumstances of the world in which we live.

3. Both subjective and objective factors are important, since the value of that which we choose is important, and also the attitude we have towards it.

4. Supposing that the objective choice is good, what is then most important is the ultimate subjective attitude—how fully we will be able to seek to serve God in the way of life.

5. Love is the greatest single determining factor in the ability to have this attitude of complete service.

Inadequate methods for discerning a vocation

Having considered the two great approaches to vocation, represented by St. Thomas and St. Ignatius, we can evaluate other more particular ways of determining a vocation, and see both the truth and value they contain, and at the same time their limitations and deficiencies. The simplified ways of discerning a vocation that we will here describe are not often proposed as though they were sufficient on their own for discerning a vocation, and rarely do those who are discerning a vocation limit themselves strictly to one of these ways. Nevertheless, the consideration of these specific ways, and of their weaknesses and deficiencies, will help us to avoid overemphasizing or misunderstanding a particular aspect of the way of discernment.

(1) Making a decision on the basis of one's own strengths and abilities

God calls each person to a way of life suited to him. Thus a plausible way of determining one's vocation is simply to determine where one's particular talents and strengths lie, to look for the way of life to which one is most suited.

The truth and value of this approach lies in its emphasis on one's personal disposition; for as we said above, given that a way of life is good, the most important factor is the way that one lives it.

There are, however, two weaknesses, or possible weaknesses, of this approach. First, it overlooks the objective superiority of certain ways of life. To be a teacher, or to serve the poor, is in itself better than to do mathematics. And therefore, in order to decide to be a mathematician, one should have more than just a particular ability for doing mathematics. There should be reason to think, first of all, that one is more, or at least equally capable of seeking holiness as a mathematician; and secondly, that the subjective advantage in favor of doing mathematics outweighs the objective superiority of being a teacher, or devoting one's life to the service of the poor.

The second possible weakness of this approach is that the subjective qualities that it considers may not be the most important. If the ability to live a way of life means the capacity to do something well, e.g., to be a good doctor or teacher, then it is important to have the ability—e.g., one should not be a doctor if he is unable to heal people—but having a greater or lesser ability is not the most important factor. Ultimately, a more important factor is the attitude one will have to the way of life. If this attitude is understood as included in one's "ability" for the life, all is well. But if this attitude is not included as part of one's "ability" for the life, then this approach is seriously deficient.

(2) Following one's inclinations

Another method that is used for deciding on a path in life, is that of following one's inclinations. There are two different reasons that may be given for this. First, there is sometimes the idea that since one is not responsible for these inclinations, they are from God, and thus are the signs God uses to indicate the path one should follow. The other reason is based on what we noted above, that the most important thing in any vocation is to devote oneself to it wholeheartedly. The idea then, is that one will devote oneself most wholeheartedly to that to which one is innerly inclined.

There is some truth to both of these ideas. However, it is a mistake either to consider inclinations in general as positive signs of God's will, or to consider such inclinations as necessary for choosing a way of life as one's vocation.

In regard to inclinations as signs of God's will, there are some inclinations that proceed more or less directly from God, either without anything intervening, or through the judgment that derives from the intimate union with God caused by charity.[2] The recognition of these inclinations belongs to the discernment of spirits described by St. Ignatius, and ideally, it is on the basis of inclinations of this kind that one makes a decision in the "second time" of St. Ignatius. These inclinations are always for our good, and ordered to God. Therefore, since God's will is for our good, these inclinations are signs of God's will. However, most of our feelings and inclinations are not of this sort, but are based on our natural and acquired character, and on our conscious and unconscious imaginations and thoughts. Hence they are not always for our good, nor always ordered to God, and so cannot be taken as signs of God's will.

The second reason for looking to one's inclinations, namely that an inner inclination to a way of life is necessary in order to embrace that way of life wholeheartedly, requires a similar distinction. In most cases, some inclination to the particular way of life should be present. However, there is no need for this inclination to be sensible rather than intellectual and spiritual. (See above, p. 36 ff.) Indeed, a sensible attraction to a way of life can present the danger that one chooses the life for natural or selfish reasons. Moreover, even a spiritual love or inclination towards the way of life considered in itself is not absolutely required. The love that ought to move someone to choose a way of life is not so much love for that way of life, as love for *God*. And for this reason it is possible for someone to embrace a way of life such as religious life, simply because it is a better way of serving God, and against his or her inclinations. St. Teresa of Avila did this: "Though I did not succeed to incline my will to being a nun, I saw that this was the best and safest state, and so, little by little, I determined to force myself to embrace it."[3] Though we should not advise everyone to follow her example, we should also not be quick to discourage others from imitating her. The Church gives us the general rule:

---

2 See ST II 45:2–4.
3 St. Teresa of Avila, *Autobiography*, Ch. 3.

"Let no one who is unwilling be driven to the pursuit of this kind of consecrated life; but, if one wishes it, let there be no one who will dissuade him, much less prevent him from undertaking it."[4]

(3) Waiting for miraculous signs

The idea of waiting for a more or less miraculous sign, or asking God for one, usually arises from the principle that we ought to choose the way of life that God wills for us, when this principle is separated from an understanding that God's will is manifested in the commandments and the counsels, in ordinary events, in the judgment of conscience, and in the inclinations of "faith working through love" (Gal 5:6). Choosing a way of life on the basis of special signs has the possible advantage of proceeding less from one's own will, and more from God's will.

This advantage of being based entirely on God's will may however be only apparent, if the choice of "signs" or the interpretation of them is colored by one's own desires—if one asks as "signs" from God things that one secretly, perhaps half-unconsciously, thinks are likely to happen; or again, if one interprets ordinary events as the fulfillment of signs. For example, a man might ask for a rose as a sign that he should propose marriage to a certain woman. If he does not ask for a specific way of getting a rose, it may already be too likely an event to be taken as in itself a sign from God. But if he then interprets the mere sight of a bouquet of roses as the fulfillment of the sign, it is evidently because he wants the "sign"; he is simply choosing what he really wants, and imagining or inventing the justification he is seeking, namely the sign from God.

The main problem with this approach does not lie in this possibility of self-deception, but in the fact that God does not usually give such extraordinary signs of his will. In regard to the priestly vocation, for example, we are told that "the voice of the

4   Pope Pius XII, *Annus Sacer*, December 8, 1950, AAS 43 (1951), 31. This rule was later taken into the general statutes for religious life; see *The General Statutes annexed to the Apostolic Constitution Sedes Sapientiae* from the Congregation for Institutes of Consecrated Life and Societies of Apostolic Life (Washington, DC: The Catholic University of America Press, 1957), Art. 32, p. 45.

Lord who is calling should not in the least be expected to come to the ears of a future priest in some extraordinary manner."[5] Such extraordinary signs of God's will are in effect sensible manifestations of God's mind, and are thus equivalent to a sensible voice from God. And while God does sometimes speak in this way to indicate his will, it is not the ordinary way. "We must not wait for the Divine Majesty to speak to us in some sensible way or that he send from heaven some Angel to point out his will for us."[6] Rather, the way God speaks to our heart is by giving it the ability to see and to cling fast to what is good. "If we always try to keep our will very firm in wanting to discover the good that has been shown to us, God will not fail to make all redound to his glory."[7] God's calling is not something external; God speaks within a person's will itself, moving it to a way of life by which that person may draw near to him. "A true vocation is nothing other than a strong, unchanging will that the person who is called possesses, so as to want to serve God in the way and in the place where the Divine Majesty calls her."[8]

(4) Attempting to draw everything from the particulars of providence

Another method used for discerning a vocation, which is related to the previous method, is that of examining the particular events in our life, in order to see where providence is leading us. The great advantage of this approach is that it helps us see the whole of our life as a continuous dialogue with God. God speaks to us in all of the events of our life, and we speak to him in all of the choices we make. And this approach is actually a good one as long as it is rightly understood.

Since all things are under the governance of God's providence, in order to consider that God's providence is guiding us to a certain choice, we must do one of two things. First, we may look for miracles of providence—i.e., things that are so improbable

---

5 Vatican Council II, *Presbyterorum Ordinis* n. 11.
6 St. Francis de Sales, *Les vrays entretiens spirituels*, 313; cf. Pope John Paul II, Homily in Benguela, June 9, 1992.
7 St. Francis de Sales, *Les vrays entretiens spirituels*, 314.
8 St. Francis de Sales, *Les vrays entretiens spirituels*, 312.

that they can be considered miraculous—which somehow signify that we ought to make a particular choice. This is then in effect the same way as the previous way; we are looking for something that externally expresses God's will for us. And so this way also has the same weaknesses and dangers as that way does.

Another way of taking guidance from divine providence, is to try to see what is good in the various possibilities presented by providence, or even determined by providence. For example, if we happen to meet repeatedly the same religious community or the same person (whom we might consider marrying), to consider whether it might be good to join that community, or marry that person. Or again, if we find ourselves for a long time unable to pursue the course that we had wanted to pursue, to consider whether it might be better to do something else. This approach is good, as long as we bear in mind that it does not determine what the better thing to do *is* (unless only one good and possible choice remains), but only draws our attention in certain directions, so that we can think and pray about those possibilities. Often God would like us to persevere in spite of difficulties, or to look beyond the good possibilities being immediately presented to us, so that we can make an even greater gift of ourselves. It is true that we should always live in the present, in the sense that we should seek to do and to act well now, but this often means having our eyes and hearts open for more than what is presently proposed to us.

If, on the other hand, we want to be led by divine providence in the sense that our judgment about what is good is to be determined simply by providence, then we will most likely end up being led by our feelings. For it is in fact impossible to depend *only* on providence, since our perception of *what* is being presented is necessarily mediated through our understanding. E.g., someone with a well-formed moral conscience, who falls in love with a woman, could see the good to pursue as the good of marriage—while someone with a poorly-formed conscience, could see the good to pursue simply as sexual intimacy. Thus, to seek to have our judgment be determined in this way by providence, will ultimately mean removing rational considerations—except for general considerations, or when something is clearly seen to be bad—and basing ourselves primarily upon feelings and emotions. For matters of importance, this is not a good way of making a decision.

84

On the other hand, when it comes to relatively unimportant decisions, it is right for our decision to be determined more by feelings than by reasons. In such matters it is not worth attempting to make a rational discernment of what is better. We may decide simply for what strikes us as good at the moment. St. Francis de Sales gives this as the solution for those who are tempted to doubt "whether it is God's will for them to do one thing rather than another: as for example, whether or not they should eat with a friend... whether they should fast on Friday or on Saturday, whether they should take recreation or abstain from it."[9] He explains:

> We should not weigh every little action to know whether it is of more value than others... It is not good service to a master to spend as much time in considering what is to be done, as in doing the things which are needful. We are to proportion our attention to the importance of what we undertake.... To what end should I put myself out to learn whether God would prefer me to say the Rosary or Our Lady's Office... to go to visit the sick in the hospital rather than to Vespers, to go to a sermon rather than to a church where there is an indulgence? Generally there is no such noteworthy importance in the one more than the other that it is needful to make any great deliberation. We must walk in good faith and without minute consideration in such matters, and, as S. Basil says, freely choose what seems to us good, so as not to weary our spirit, lose time, and put ourselves in danger of disquiet, scruples, and superstition. But I mean always where there is no great disproportion between the two works, and where there is no considerable circumstance on one side more than on the other.[10]

Proposal for discernment of vocation

"Above all these put on love, which binds everything together in perfect harmony." (Col 3:14) Every choice of a state of life, every discernment of a particular vocation, should be placed in the context of the goal of Christian life, which is the perfection of the love of God and neighbor.

---

9 *Treatise on the Love of God*, Bk. 8, Ch. 14.
10 Ibid., 105–7.

Hence, what we must strive for above all, prior to "discerning" our vocation, or "deciding" on a state of life, is to purify our heart, to truly love and to seek God above all and in all things, and to carry this attitude of love into our choice of a state of life. This purity of heart is the key to making a good choice. If we possess this purity of heart, we can be confident of choosing well, of finding God's will for us; if we do not possess it, we are in danger of settling upon our own will in place of God's will. St. Alphonsus states:

> It is necessary for you to pray diligently to God to make you know his will as to what state he wants you in. But take notice that to have this light, you must pray to him with indifference. He who prays to God to enlighten him in regard to a state of life, but without indifference, and who, instead of conforming to the divine will, would sooner have God conform to his will, is like a pilot that pretends to wish his ship to advance, but in reality does not want it to: he throws his anchor into the sea, and then unfurls his sails. God neither gives light nor speaks his word to such persons. But if you entreat him with indifference and resolution to follow his will, God will make you know clearly what state is better for you.[11]

But after striving to purify our heart, and asking God to guide and enlighten our choice, we must then take the means necessary to make a good choice. For God does not usually enlighten us in such a way as to make it unnecessary for us to deliberate about what we choose, but rather enlightens us precisely in our deliberation about the choice we are to make.

We can here distinguish three general means for making this choice, three ways of determining which way of life is the best way for us to grow in love of God and neighbor, and to bring others closer to God: (1) Reason; (2) Love; (3) Providence.

The first means for determining a way of life is the prudent consideration of reason, weighing the various factors and the various possibilities, and making a judgment as to which possibility provides the best means for living love and growing in it in one's concrete circumstances and conditions. This way of making a

---

11 St. Alphonsus, "Sull'utilità degli esercizi spirituali fatti in solitudine," *Opere Ascetiche*, Vol. 3 (Torino: Pier Giacinto Marietti), 616.

decision includes the second and third, inasmuch as this consideration takes into account the loves one possesses, just as it takes into account one's other dispositions, and it takes into account the workings of providence, just as it takes into account particular events and circumstances in one's life and in the world. Because it includes the second and third ways, and because a choice not made through prudence has a greater danger of being erroneous, when, and to the extent that it is possible to make a decision in this first way, it is the preferable way.

Sometimes one can make a judgment that some general form or way of life is the better means, but cannot make a concrete conclusion—and so this judgment leads to an intention, but not yet to the choice of a particular way of life. For example, one may judge that religious life is the best way for one, while one is still unable to judge which religious order one should enter. Or one might judge that he should marry, but not yet know whom he should marry.

The second means for determining a way of life is love; when one is unable to make a judgment of reason as to the best way of life, and when the inability to come to a conclusion based on reason cannot be reasonably resolved by the advice of a wiser person, then a choice can be made on the basis of love. One may and normally should choose that which he loves more. Other things being equal, he will be able to devote himself more perfectly and intensely to that which he loves more, and therefore will live that way of life better. Often the concrete choice of a particular religious order is made almost entirely on the basis of love, and even more so the choice of a particular man or woman in marriage.

The third means for determining a way of life is divine providence. Now, as noted above, there are several ways in which divine providence can play a role in choosing a way of life. (See page 82 ff.) First, one relies on divine providence when one makes a choice by one of the first two means. In this case, one is primarily trusting in divine providence to bring the right evidence to one's attention, or to direct one's love, rather than considering the path of divine providence itself.

A second way in which a way of life may be found by divine providence is when providence determines the way of life. Thus, if one believed that one was called to religious life, but due to an incurable case of severe depression, one was unable to enter religious life, then one should accept this as God's will, and turn one's attention to other ways of life. Or again, someone might believe that he should marry, but find himself unable to do so. In such a case, he could then accept the situation as appointed by divine providence, and embrace the single state as a means of serving God and neighbor. Thus Pope Pius XII, speaking of the various ways in which a vocation to virginity may be experienced, includes the example of a woman who wants to marry, but is unable to do so.

> When one thinks upon the maidens and the women who voluntarily renounce marriage in order to consecrate themselves to a higher life of contemplation, of sacrifice, and of charity, a luminous word comes immediately to the lips: vocation!... This vocation, this call of love, makes itself felt in very diverse manners... But also the young Christian woman, remaining unmarried in spite of herself, who nevertheless trusts in the providence of the heavenly Father, recognizes in the vicissitudes of life the voice of the Master: "*Magister adest et vocat te*" (John 11:28); It is the master, and he is calling you! She responds, she renounces the beloved dream of her adolescence and her youth: to have a faithful companion in life, to form a family! And in the impossibility of marriage she recognizes her vocation; then, with a broken but submissive heart, she also gives her whole self to more noble and diverse good works.[12]

The third way in which providence may guide one to a way of life, is when one's way is not determined by providence, but one makes one's choice directly on the basis of divine providence. E.g., someone might make a specific choice because in God's providence, that choice is presented to him here and now, or because it has been presented to him several times through unusual coincidences. Perhaps several people, without any apparent reason, have suggested the same course to a person: that he enter a seminary, or that he consider marriage. Or perhaps he once thought of joining a religious community, and over a period of years,

---

12 Pope Pius XII, *Address to Italian Women*, October 21, 1945, AAS 37 (1945), 287.

happens simply by chance to meet different members of that community in various circumstances. If these events are used simply as occasions for considering such a possible way of life, or are simply occasions when one realizes how much one wants to pursue such a way of life, then one would fundamentally be making the choice in one of the first two ways, by thought or by love. But what we are now considering is the case in which one chooses a way or state of life precisely because he sees it as presented to him by providence, the case in which a person would, for example, finally make up his mind to enter a community or seminary, just because of coincidences such as these.

Generally speaking, this third way of using providence to make an important choice should be employed only to the extent that the other ways are insufficient. For since everything is finally to be attributed to divine providence, that which is particularly attributed to divine providence is restricted to that which has no created cause, or in other words, that which happens by chance. Hence, to look to divine providence *alone* in order to make one's choice, would be analogous to making a decision by throwing dice. And therefore this should also be done with similar reasons and in a way similar to the way in which one would make a decision by chance, asking God to guide the chance event. Regarding the process of making a decision by means of something that in itself happens by chance, St. Thomas Aquinas lays down four cautions:

> [If the outcome of lots] is expected from God... then using lots in this way is not evil in itself, as Augustine says. Nevertheless this may be sinful in four ways. First, if one have recourse to lots without any necessity, for this seems to be a way of putting God to the test....
>
> Secondly, even when there is a necessity, if someone uses lots without reverence. Hence Bede says, "If compelled by some necessity, people think that God should be consulted by means of lots, following the example of the Apostles, let them note that the Apostles did not do this except after gathering together the assembly of the brethren and pouring out prayers to God" (Super Act. Apost. i).
>
> Thirdly, if divine oracles are used for earthly affairs...

Fourthly, if people use lots in ecclesiastical elections, which should be made by the inspiration of the Holy Spirit. Hence, as Bede says, "before Pentecost, Matthias was chosen by lot to be ordained," namely because the fullness of the Holy Spirit was not yet poured out in the Church, "while the seven deacons were afterwards ordained not by lot, but by the choice of the disciples."... But if necessity presses, then it is licit to implore the divine judgment with lots, keeping due reverence.[13]

Similarly, a decision should be made directly on the basis of providence only when it is an important decision for a spiritual good, only when it is necessary, that is, when a decision cannot be made in other ways; and it should be made in prayer.

As to the ways of making a decision on the basis of providence, there are different ways of doing so, as we noted above. Any one of these ways may be used, as long as one does not choose the way of making a choice so as to determine in advance a particular outcome. If one is to be guided simply by providence in making a choice, then one cannot do so in such a way as to give oneself an answer actually predetermined by oneself.

Confirmation of a Choice

As was noted above in the section "Devotion to the Lord" (p. 8 ff.), an essential factor in one's vocation is the dedication or commitment with which one commits oneself to a way of life, how wholeheartedly one devotes oneself to the practice of the love of God and neighbor in that way of life. For this reason, it is important that a strong and firm intention follow upon one's choice. The perception of this firm intention for the service of God in a way of life results in a certain peace. And for this reason, the possession of peace in one's heart in regard to a particular choice is often considered the confirming sign of the correctness of one's choice. Inner peace may even be called *the* sign of a vocation.

One caution, however, should be made about the use of peace as a confirmation of one's vocation, or the lack of peace as an indication that one should not pursue a particular way of life. On

---

13 ST II-II 95:8.

the one hand, there can be a superficial peace that is the result of blindness deriving from one's emotions. For example, a Catholic woman who falls in love with a Christian man who is strongly opposed to the Catholic Church, may feel peace at the idea of marrying him, even when it would be unwise for her to do so. The emotions connected with spousal love are powerful, and can strongly influence one's judgment. On the other hand, one can feel a certain disquiet and lack of peace even when one is doing one's best to act according to one's conscience. For example, a employee may finally feel obliged in conscience to refuse to perform dishonest business practices; he may be worried about being fired, and how he will support his family. And especially if it is not clear beyond all possible doubt that the questionable practices are ultimately dishonest, he may feel torn inside, wondering whether he made the right decision. This kind of lack of peace is not necessarily a sign that one is not following God's will.

Thus, peace can be used as a sign that one has made the right choice, or is following the right path, but it must be rightly understood. The peace one should have is the quiet of the heart that follows upon a trust in God together with the conviction that one is acting for God and in accordance with God's will, *to the extent* that it is possible for a particular person to have this conviction in a particular situation. Some persons are by nature and upbringing disposed to question what they have done and are doing; such persons will not generally experience so complete a feeling of peace, even when they are acting well, and have made the right decision. Again, some situations do not allow for a strong feeling of certainty, and in these situations the conviction of acting well, and therefore the corresponding peace will tend to be less perceptible.

A good spiritual director can be of much help in distinguishing such a true and deep peace from a superficial peace, and generally, in guiding us as we decide upon our path in life. He can often see things which we would not notice on our own, and assist us in hearing and following the voice of the true spiritual director, Jesus. For this reason, though in many cases it is not easy, we should make a real effort to find a holy and wise person who is willing to be our spiritual director.

Summary

In summary, we should begin by considering God's eternal love, and how to respond to that love. If after thinking about and reflecting on all the relevant factors, we can see what the best means is for practicing love and growing in it, then we should choose that means. Otherwise, among the various means that we can see would be good means for practicing love and growing in it, we should choose the means to which we are more inclined—not according to a quickly passing inclination, but a deep or abiding inclination, that is, according to true love. If this too is insufficient, then we may look at the situation in which we happen to find ourselves, or the coincidences that suggest a choice to us, and from among the possible good choices, choose that which seems most of all suggested.

As we reflect and choose a way of life, we should always bear in mind that the path we choose is in the end not a path of our own invention, but is part of God's design; each of us is in a particular place in the world, so that we may choose a particular path to God. And so, after choosing a path for our life, we should gratefully give thanks to God for his love, and the opportunity and invitation to love him that he has offered to us.

The method of finding one's vocation that has been presented here, should not be taken as a hard and fast rule for how to proceed in deciding upon one's path in life. It is meant as a kind of help, not something that needs to be rigorously adhered to in every case. Between the way of proceeding presented by St. Thomas, to that presented by St. Ignatius, there are many different intermediary ways that one may follow. What matters most is purifying our hearts, sincerely striving for an ever greater love, and while always being obedient to the teachings and precepts of the Church and observing Christian prudence, being at the same time open to the movements of the Holy Spirit, wherever he may lead us. Seeking and pursuing our vocation should be neither a mechanical nor an anxiety-filled procedure, but a living and joyful journey with God! "God is greater than our hearts, and he knows everything" (1 John 3:20).

Selected Bibliography

Scripture

Holy Bible, Revised Standard Version, Catholic Edition. San Francisco: Ignatius Press, 1966.

Reference Works

Catechismus Catholicae Ecclesiae. Città del Vaticano: Libreria Editrice Vaticana, 1997.

Catholic Encyclopedia. Edited by Charles Herbermann et al. New York: The Encyclopedia Press, 1913–14.

Code of Canon Law, Latin-English Edition. Washington DC: Canon Law Society of America, 1983.

Denzinger, Henry, *Enchiridion symbolorum*, 36th Edition. Rome: Herder, 1976

The States of Perfection, edited by the Benedictine monks of Solesmes, translated by Mother E. O'Gorman, R.S.C.J. Boston: The Daughters of St. Paul, 1967.

94

Primary sources

Alphonsus de Liguori, St., *Opera omnia*, online at
        http://www.intratext.com.

——————— *Theologia moralis*, Ed. P. Leonardi Gaudé,
        vols. 2 and 4. Rome: Typographia Vaticana,
        1907 and 1912.

Aquinas, Thomas, St., *Sancti Thomae Aquinatis doctoris
        angelici Opera omnia iussu Leonis XIII. O. M.
        edita,* cura et studio fratrum praedicatorum.
        Rome: 1882–. Vols. 4–12, *Summa theologiae.*
        Vols. 13–15, *Summa contra gentiles.* Vol. 25,
        Quaestiones de quolibet. Vol. 41, *Contra
        impugnantes, De perfectione spiritualis vitae,
        Contra doctrinam retrahentium.* Vol. 42

——————— *Scriptum super libros Sententiarum.* Vols. 1
        and 2 (containing Books I and II), ed. P.
        Mandonnet. Paris: Lethielleux, 1929. Vols. 3
        and 4 (containing Books III and IV, up to IV,
        dist. 22), ed. Maria Fabianus Moos. Paris:
        Lethielleux, 1933 and 1947.

——————— *Quaestiones disputatae.* 2 vols. Ed. P. Bazzi,
        M. Calcaterra et al. Turin/Rome: Marietti,
        1965.

——————— *Super Epistolas sancti Pauli lectura.* 2 vols.
        Ed. P. Raphaelis Cai. Turin/Rome: Marietti,
        1953.

——————— *Sancti Thomae Aquinatis Opera omnia ut sunt
        in Indice Thomistico.* 7 vols. Ed. Robert
        Busa, Vol. 6: *Reportationes*

——————— *Super Evangelium sancti Ioannis lectura.* Ed.
        P. Raphaelis Cai. Turin-Rome: Marietti, 1952.

Balthasar, Hans Urs Von, *Christlicher Stand*. Einsiedeln: Johannes Verlag, 1977.

Benedict, St., *Regula sancti benedicti*, PL 66:215–932.

Francis De Sales, St., *Traitté de l'amour de Dieu*, in *Œuvres de S. François de Sales*, Vols. 4–5. Annecy: Monastère de la Visitation, 1894. Translated by Rev. Henry Mackey, OSB, as *Treatise on the Love of God.* Rockford: Tan Books, 1997.

—————— *Les vrays entretiens spirituels*; *Œuvres de S. François de Sales*, Vol. 6. Annecy: Monastère de la Visitation, 1894.

Ignatius of Loyola, St., *Letters of St. Ignatius of Loyola*, Translated by William J. Young, S.J. Chicago: Loyola University Press, 1959.

—————— *Sancti Ignatii de Loyola exercitia spiritualia*, in *Monumenta historica Societatis Iesu*, Series 2, Vol. 1. Rome: Institutum Historicum Societatis Iesu, 1969.

—————— *Directoria exercitiorum spiritualium,* in *Monumenta Ignatiana*, Series 2, Vol. 2. Rome: Monumenta Historica Societatis Iesu, 1955. Many of these texts are translated by Martin E. Palmer, S.J., in *On Giving the Spiritual Exercises: The Early Jesuit Manuscript Directories and the Official Directory of 1599.* St. Louis: The Institute of Jesuit Sources, 1996.

—————— *The Spiritual Exercises of St. Ignatius*, Translated by Fr. Elder Mullan, S.J. New York: P.J. Kenedy & Sons, 1914.

———————— *The Spiritual Exercises of St. Ignatius: A New Translation Based on Studies in the Language of the Autograph*, translated by Louis J. Puhl, S.J. Chicago: Loyola University Press, 1951.

John Paul II, Pope, *Insegnamenti di Giovanni Paolo II*. Rome: Libreria Editrice Vaticana.

———————— *The Teachings of Pope John Paul II*, CD-ROM. Salem, OR, Harmony Media, 2002.

Paul VI, Pope, *Insegnamenti di Paolo VI.* Rome: Tipografia Poliglotta Vaticana.

Congregation for Institutes of Consecrated Life and Societies of Apostolic Life, *The General Statues annexed to the Apostolic Constitution Sedes Sapientiae*, promulgated by Pope Pius XII on May 31, 1956. Washington DC: The Catholic University of America Press, 1957.

———————— *Religiosorum institutio*, Instruction on the Careful Selection And Training Of Candidates For The States Of Perfection And Sacred Orders, February 2, 1961, English translation in Canon Law Digest, Bouscaren & O'Connor, Vol. 5. Milwaukee: Bruce Publishing Company, 1963, 452–86.

Teresa of Avila, St., *Obras completas*, 4th Edition. Edited by Alberto Barrientos. Madrid: Editorial de Espiritualidad, 1994.

Thérèse of Lisieux, St., *Œuvres complètes*. De Brouwer: Éditions du Cerf & Desclée, 1992.

Wojtyła, Karol,   *Love & Responsibility*, 2nd edition. San
              Francisco: Ignatius Press, 1993. Translated
              from *Miłość i odpowiedzialność*. Lublin:
              Towarzystwo Naukowe KUL, 2001.

Vatican Council II, *Constitutiones, decreta, declarationes.*
              Rome: Libreria Editrice Vaticana, 1993.

Secondary Sources

Berthier, Rev. J., *States of the Christian Life and Vocation.*
              New York: P. O'Shea, 1879.

Butler, Fr. Richard, O.P., *Religious Vocation: An Unnecessary
              Mystery.* Rockford: Tan Books, 2005.

De Caussade, S.J., *Self-Abandonment to Divine Providence.*
              Translated by Algar Thorold. Rockford: Tan
              Books and Publishers, 1987.

Doyle, Fr. William, S.J., *Vocations.* Dublin: Irish messenger,
              1873.

Dubay, Thomas, S.M. *Authenticity: a Biblical Theology of
              Discernment.* New Jersey: Dimension Books,
              1976.

————————   *And You Are Christ's: The Charism of
              Virginity and the Celibate Life.* San
              Francisco: Ignatius Press, 1987.

Farrell, Edward P., *The Theology of Religious Vocation.* St.
              Louis: Herder, 1952.

Hardon, Fr. John, *The Retreat Election.* Online at
              http://www.therealpresence.org/archives/Chris
              tian_Spirituality.htm

Heris, Charles V., O.P., *Spirituality of Love*. Translated by David Martin. St. Louis and London: Herder, 1965.

Schleck, Charles A., C.S.C, *The Theology of Vocations*. Milwaukee: Bruce Publishing Company, 1963.

Unger, Fr. Dominic J., OFM, *The Mystery of Love for the Single*. Rockford: Tan Books and Publishers, 2005.

Vignat, Louis, S.J., *La vocation a la vie religieuse*. Translated by Matthew L. Fortier, S.J., as *In Thy Courts*. London: Longmans, 1907.

Von Speyr, Adrienne, *They Followed His Call: Vocations and Asceticism*. Translated by Erasmo Leiva Merikakis. San Francisco: Ignatius Press, 2000.

Made in the USA
Middletown, DE
05 August 2021